REFLECTIONS ON
TSUDA
UMEKO

JAPAN LIBRARY

REFLECTIONS ON
TSUDA UMEKO

Pioneer of Women's Education in Japan

OBA Minako

Translated by TANI Yu

Japan Publishing Industry Foundation for Culture

Note:
This book follows the Hepburn system of romanization. Except for words in the English dictionary and common place names, long vowels are indicated by macrons. The tradition of placing the family name first has been followed for Japanese names.

Reflections on Tsuda Umeko: Pioneer of Women's Education in Japan
Ōba Minako. Translated by Tani Yū.

Published by
Japan Publishing Industry Foundation for Culture (JPIC)
2-2-30 Kanda-Jinbocho, Chiyoda-ku, Tokyo 101-0051, Japan

First English edition: March 2021
English publishing rights arranged with SHOGAKUKAN, Tokyo.

© 1990, 2019 Tani Yū
English translation © 2021 Tani Yū

This book is a translation of *Tsuda Umeko* (P + D Books, SHOGAKUKAN, 2019), which was originally published by Asahi Shimbun Publications Inc. in 1990.

Book design: Miki Kazuhiko, Ampersand Works

Printed and bound in Japan
ISBN 978-4-86658-181-1
https://japanlibrary.jpic.or.jp/

CONTENTS

PREFACE TO THE ENGLISH EDITION

Tsuda Umeko, who lived from 1864 to 1929, was a pioneer in women's education and an iconic figure of modern Japanese history—iconic enough to be chosen as the face of Japan's new five-thousand-yen banknote, set to go into circulation in 2024. The decision to give Japan's currency a new look is what led to the present volume: an English translation of a book written by Ōba Minako more than thirty years ago.

One hundred and thirty years ago, in 1871, five Japanese girls—ages six to fifteen—boarded a ship in Yokohama to join a group of eminent men referred to as the Iwakura Mission. Led by the high-ranking statesman Iwakura Tomomi, the mission was embarking on a two-year tour of the United States and Europe, entrusted by the Japanese government with the task of renegotiating treaties with Western nations and observing and learning from those nations so that Japan could modernize itself as quickly and efficiently as possible. Members included government ministers, numerous high officials, and many scholars. Accompanying the group were several dozen students assigned to study in the U.S., Britain, France, Germany, and Russia. All of them were men, except for the five girls mentioned above.

In the decade leading up to the Iwakura Mission, numerous Japanese had been sent to the West to scout out the land, so to speak. Those who went to America were impressed not only by the technology and fine machines, but also by the country's democratic ideals, its great energy, and its innovative spirit. The more observant among them noticed that American women—especially those they met in the company of powerful men—were well educated, well-spoken, and capable of interacting with men as equals. Women like these would be needed if Japan wanted to do business with the West, they thought. Such women would be staunch helpmates to their husbands and wise mothers who could raise strong and capable sons. This reasoning led to an interesting plan: in order to jump-start the new "breed" of woman, the government would send a number of girls with the Iwakura Mission. They must be young enough to learn and absorb the English language and American customs to perfection, and after ten years of study in the United States, they would return to Japan to teach other women what they had learned.

Tsuda Umeko was the youngest of the girls. When she boarded the ship she was not quite seven, which was younger than the originators of the plan had in mind, but the five were the only ones to volunteer (or rather, to be volunteered by their parents or guardians). In any event, the two oldest—who were fifteen—were not flexible enough to adapt to a foreign land and returned to Japan within a year. The remaining three, Yamakawa Sutematsu (eleven), Nagai Shigeko (nine), and Tsuda Umeko, fulfilled their mission and returned to Japan a decade later.

Unfortunately, in the eleven years after the girls' departure, the political atmosphere in Japan had changed. The country was undergoing a backlash against Westernization and modernization, and the politician who played a leading role in dispatching the girls was temporarily out of power. The girls were welcomed home warmly enough, but quietly forgotten and politely ignored. Male students sent abroad in the same way were prized for their newly acquired knowledge and given important posts, but the government had no use for the girls. Yamakawa and Nagai accepted this reality and soon married, but Tsuda Umeko held fast to the idea that had been drummed into her head from early childhood: her mission in life was to share the knowledge she had gained in America with the women of her native land.

Carefully thinking and rethinking her specific goals and strategy, she slowly won the trust of people who would support her. She taught, studied, and gained new qualifications. She asked for help when necessary, and in 1900, eighteen years after her return from America, succeeded in founding a private school. It was, just as she intended, a school that provided women with the knowledge and training necessary to lead independent lives. This school was the precursor of Tsuda College (present-day Tsuda University), a highly respected institution of higher learning for women.

Umeko's success as an educator made her one of the most respected and well-known women of the Meiji era, but little was known of her private life. Although bold and decisive in her actions, Umeko was a quiet woman, not given to openly expressing her private thoughts. However, in 1984 a trunk full of old papers was discovered in an attic of one of the buildings at the college, and they turned out to be personal letters—more than four hundred of them—written by Umeko over three decades to Adeline Lanman, her foster mother in America. Charles and Adeline Lanman, a childless couple with connections to the Japanese legation in Washington, D.C., had taken Umeko into their home and loved and cared for her like a daughter for eleven years. From the time she returned to Japan in 1882 until Adeline's death in 1914, Umeko faithfully wrote long and confiding letters, describing her experiences in great detail, expressing opinions sometimes withheld from her own parents, and developing ideas about making a place for herself in a land that had become strange to her. The letters reveal a fine intellect and keen eye for detail, and provide a remarkable portrait of life in the Meiji era in addition to shedding light on the writer herself. They are all the more interesting for being written by a native Japanese who became a semi-outsider through an accident of history.

Shortly after the discovery of the letters, Ōba Minako, the author of this book, was commissioned to weave them into a biographical sketch of Tsuda Umeko. Ōba was an established writer, but she was known primarily for her novels and had never written a biography. She was recommended for the project because she was a graduate of Tsuda College, familiar with Umeko's educational ideals, and because she too had lived in America for more than ten years. The idea was to write Umeko's story from the viewpoint of a writer who had shared her experience of living with two languages and two cultures, and as one of the many students who had benefited from Umeko's passionate determination to build a school where women could learn to take a responsible place in society. In short, it was to be a personal story—the story of Tsuda Umeko as a person, written by a writer with a personal connection to the school that Umeko founded.

Reading the letters, Ōba was charmed by Umeko's writing, fascinated by her mind, and impressed by her stubborn campaign to educate Japanese women. Being a writer by profession, Ōba was particularly interested in the way that Umeko's mind—its wide horizons, its flexibility, its ability to reason fairly and without prejudice—was informed by her intimacy with two languages. She felt new respect for Umeko as an educator after realizing that Umeko had placed English at the center of the school curriculum not only because it could provide women with a useful tool for entering the work force. Her deeper objective was to offer them a wider vision of the world—a vision that comes to a person through learning to use a foreign language.

Languages have great power over an individual. A language exists before we do, and we must accept its rules and its meanings if we wish to share in its power. On the other hand, to share means to possess a doorway into a whole new world. Umeko met and spoke with Helen Keller in 1898 and was deeply moved by Helen's account of how she rediscovered language and how it changed her world. Encounter with a first language is no doubt of paramount importance, but Umeko possessed two languages, and she knew from experience that different languages and cultures have slightly (or greatly) different ways of looking at the world, and that each language and culture has a different way of giving shape to a person's thoughts. Japanese and English have different perspectives on the world, and to possess both means to possess two perspectives. However, in order for individuals to master a language, they must learn it through personal effort. Proficiency in a language cannot be bought or borrowed. And because each person brings something different to the act of learning—different aptitudes, a different temperament, a different past, different needs—each act of education should also be, in essence, personal and individual. This was another important aspect of Umeko's idea of education, and it is for this reason that she wanted Tsuda College to be a small, intimate school.

History also has great power over an individual. Unlike language, it cannot be learned as a skill or mastered, but some people change it more than others. Tsuda Umeko probably became an educator through an accident of history. After all, the six-year-old child clearly had little choice in the matter when she was taken to America, and those who sent her do not seem to have had any clear strategy in mind. But she took what destiny offered her and made a notable contribution to Japanese history by working passionately for the rest of her life to educate and improve the lives of the women who came after her. Many people today, not only women, and not only those who attended her school, walk in her footsteps without knowing it.

Ōyama Sutematsu (formerly Yamakawa Sutematsu), who sailed with Tsuda Umeko to America and remained a close friend and ally throughout her life, died of pneumonia during the flu epidemic of 1919. This seems to me another poignant reminder that the story of Tsuda Umeko and her generation is not just a story of long, long ago. It is part of a history that we are still living.

The project to translate this book into English was launched in January 2020, around the time that COVID-19 made its way to Japan. JPIC, publisher of the Japan Library series that this volume has the honor of joining, put together a fine team to support my translation effort: Patricia Fister, Saka Chihiro, and Shiraishi Eri. There was mention in the beginning of having a face-to-face meeting "once the pandemic is over," but the world did not quite reach that phase before the project was completed. The three members of the team remain faceless to me, although I have some idea of their minds from the comments we exchanged in the margins of countless computer files. I am sorry I was never able to meet them, but I am very grateful for their meticulous perusal of my manuscript, their pertinent corrections and advice, and the much-needed knowledge they shared with me.

I would like to extend a special thank you to Takahashi Yūko, president of Tsuda University, for contributing a commentary to this volume, and for permitting us access to the original English text of Tsuda Umeko's letters. Because Ōba Minako referred to the original transcripts of Umeko's letters when writing this book and utilized (in Japanese translation) portions not included in the published English selection of her correspondence, we had to ask the staff of the university reference section to search through hundreds of pages of transcripts for the missing excerpts. This was an undeniably daunting task, and I am particularly indebted to Nakada Yuki, who shouldered much of the burden.

Many thanks also to Kuno Akiko, great granddaughter of Ōyama Sutematsu, who was kind enough to provide us with the original text of letters written by Sutematsu to her friend Alice Bacon. Also to Ōue Asami, who edited the original Japanese text of this book when it first appeared in serial form in *Gekkan Asahi* (a monthly journal published by Asahi Shimbun) and provided information that only she could give.

Last but not least, I would like to express my gratitude to JPIC for selecting this book for the Japan Library series and making it available to an English-reading audience. Special thanks go to JPIC editor Sawada Haruna, who coordinated a project that was complicated to begin with and made more so by the COVID-19 pandemic. I am told that she is a graduate of Tsuda University, and having steeped myself in the story of Tsuda Umeko for many months, I am certain that her diligence and ability owe something to the excellence of her education.

Finally, designers Miki Kazuhiko and Hayashi Miyoko at Ampersand Works painstakingly gave the book the physical shape that we proudly present to the world. As Ōba wrote toward the end of this book, it takes a great deal of work by a great many people to bring even one modest book to publication. Once again, I thank each and every collaborator and contributor.

Tani Yū
January 2021

Tsuda Umeko (1901)
Photo courtesy of Tsuda University.

CHAPTER
1
RETURN

Sunday
November 19, 1882[1]

One day more of traveling. We are nearly there, and this is the last I shall write, before we see our own, dear Japan and meet those so near and yet so unknown. We have only two hundred forty-six miles more to go after this noon, and, of course, unless something serious happens to prevent it, we will be there in twenty-four hours, and probably about midday, which is just what we want, as I would like to see the entrance of the bay and the approaching land and Fujiyama. Today the weather is perfectly glorious, cool, bracing with the brightest blue sky, and deep blue water calm and still like a mill pond. There is hardly any motion, and I have been sunning myself on deck with feelings more easily imagined than described.

Oh, if we had only had more such days, how enchanting the voyage would have been. I shut my eyes and say, "Can it be possible such a day ever came and went before?" And then the idea of what tomorrow will bring me, and seeing Shige, and the ending of this trip makes me almost wild, when it suddenly rushes over me like a wave, and I realize it all in a moment. Yes, the long trip is over and I am far away indeed. Sutematsu and I awoke this morning and said, "Just

1   Tsuda Umeko's letters are quoted from transcripts of the original correspondence, made after 1984 when the letters were rediscovered. The letters were compiled, edited, and published as *The Attic Letters: Ume Tsuda's Correspondence to Her American Mother* (Furuki Yoshiko et al., eds., New York: Weatherhill, 1991). We gratefully quote from this volume wherever possible, but because the *The Attic Letters* is a selection from the whole correspondence, some of the portions cited by Ōba Minako could not be found in the book. In the latter case, the original transcripts were referred to. Many thanks to those at Tsuda University who undertook the formidable task of locating the missing texts.

think only one more day—only twenty-four hours." I am wild with joy and can hardly contain myself—next moment I am filled with strange misgivings. If I could only speak my own language, it would be so much easier for me.

The time so often dreamed of, and imagined, is close by. With the most interested occupation I turn around and say, "We are almost there," to Sutematsu. When we first came on board three weeks seemed so far, so distant, but now it has come and gone, though slowly, yet not realizable. You can imagine my face as red as a beet from now onward, from excitement. . . .

Tomorrow turns a new page in my life. May it be a good one.

Tsuda Umeko wrote this letter on November 19, 1882 (the 15th year of Meiji), sitting in her cabin on board the *Arabic*, which had sailed from San Francisco and was about to enter the port of Yokohama. Umeko was one of five girls dispatched to study in the United States eleven years earlier, under the sponsorship of the Meiji government and the Hokkaido Development Commission.[2] The Shige and Sutematsu mentioned in the letter are Nagai Shigeko and Yamakawa Sutematsu, also members of the group.

The five girls pose in Western dress for the first time. Left to right: Nagai Shigeko, Ueda Teiko, Yoshimasu Ryōko, Tsuda Umeko, and Yamakawa Sutematsu. (Chicago, 1872)

Photo courtesy of Tsuda University.

---

2 The Japanese name for this office was "Hokkaido Kaitakushi." In Umeko's time it was called the Hokkaido Colonization Office, but the translation was later changed to Hokkaido Development Commission. The latter is a more literal translation since *kaitaku* is Japanese for "development" or "breaking new ground."

Shige had returned to Japan the year before, and Sutematsu—later the wife of Ōyama Iwao[3]—was the only one on board the *Arabic* with Umeko as she returned to Japan. The other two girls of the original five had gone home soon after their arrival in America for health reasons and were unable to complete their planned course of study. Those girls were already fifteen when they left Japan and probably unable to adapt to life in a strange land. Tsuda Umeko was the youngest of the girls, being only seven years old when she arrived in America. She spent eleven years there and was now nearly eighteen. Umeko was born in 1864 on December 3 (December 31 by the modern calendar[4]), which means that she celebrated her eighteenth birthday shortly after her return to Japan.

Ever since she began her long trip home, Umeko had been writing diary-like letters to Adeline Lanman, wife of Charles Lanman. The couple had taken Umeko into their home and cherished her like a

Tsuda Umeko at the age of seven, shortly after her arrival in Washington, D.C. (1872)
Photo courtesy of Tsuda University.

Adeline Lanman, Umeko's beloved American mother. (Date unknown)
Photo courtesy of Tsuda University.

---

3   Ōyama Iwao (1842–1916) was a military officer who became one of the founders of the Imperial Japanese Army.

4   The traditional calendar was an adjusted lunar calendar. Japan officially adopted the Gregorian calendar in 1873, but both calendars remained in use until 1909, which makes it difficult to pinpoint dates from that era.

daughter during her eleven years in America. Charles Lanman accompanied Umeko and Sutematsu from his home in Georgetown, Washington D.C., to Chicago, where he placed them in the care of Professor J.D. Davis[5] of Kyoto's Dōshisha School, as Davis was about to return to Japan.

After parting from Mrs. Lanman, Umeko wrote to her continually—on the train from the east coast to the west coast, and on the ship from San Francisco to Tokyo. Four days after her arrival, she wrote:

Thursday
November 23, 1882

Oh, Mrs. Lanman, everyone is so kind and considerate. I thank God for all His blessings. Many things I have to tell you, but firstly it is so lovely to have a Christian home to come to. Before every meal grace is said and after breakfast we have a chapter read in Japanese, verse by verse all around, then hymn and prayer. Oh, how much better is my lot than the others'! When we arrived in the depot from Yokohama, eleven of them from our house met me and gave me such a hearty welcome home. At the house were gathered many relatives and since my arrival a great many come every day bringing presents of candy, fish, *kakis* [persimmons], to me and all congratulating my return. I am so busy seeing them, that I have but little time and can only write when I come up to bed and all is quiet and shut up. Father gets letters of congratulations on my arrival and, according to an ancient custom when a great event occurs, the rice is cooked with red beans; my mother has had some for us. So you see my return is a great thing.

You would be astonished to see how easily we Japanese take to Japanese ways. I now bow low to everybody and have to sit on the

---

5   An American missionary and one of Dōshisha's founding members.

floor and talk, though we have a foreign parlor with chairs. At meals we also sit at table instead of on the floor.

The Japanese food tastes very nice and I have taken to it as naturally as fish to water, but at every meal there is bread and something foreign for me as they don't want me to get sick. They wanted to sugar and milk my tea and have butter for bread, but I would not let them. All the things I eat, the taste comes back and is as natural as possible. Is it not strange after so long a time?

. . . The hardest thing is the taking off the shoes. My sister had kindly knitted socks for me and these I put on, but I don't feel comfortable in them, and it is the greatest nuisance to have to button and unbutton every time you go anywhere but it is absolutely necessary as our heels would not only ruin the mattings, but scratch the wood work. I shall get accustomed to this as well as the sitting down [on the floor]. I can't yet sit down polite fashion, but they don't make me at all.

Our house is in the country[6] and I am so glad. It is not large and I have an upstairs room from which I can see Fujiyama on clear days. The ground around is highly cultivated and I shall have all the vegetables I want. My father has a bedstead for me and I have linen underneath, but a Japanese cover over, and I like it so much. It is so much lighter and warmer than American things. I have a table and an improvised washstand with basin. My father says he intended getting me furniture but was so busy he could not. My things in the trunk are in dire confusion, and I must get some place for them. However, one thing at first and then another. They do many extra things for me and I must not ask for too much.

What a crowd of little folks we have here! The children are so cunning and I think I can learn from them many Japanese words. . . .

---

6   In Azabu, which is no longer in the country but in central Tokyo.

I spent one night at Shige's home. Her house is very nice and is all Japanese, but her room, and that is very nicely fixed, is in American style. The night I went, Sutematsu was there, and we talked a long while in bed. They dressed me in Japanese clothes and you don't know how funny I looked. Then I took a Japanese hot bath, which would be very odd to you all, but which is very neat and pleasant. Shige is a great help, for she tells us what to do, and what not, and Koto[7] does too, for Japanese etiquette is so strict and I am in fear all the time of making a bad blunder and of being unintentionally rude. For an instance, one must never leave any uneaten rice at meals when dining out—not a kernel even. How different from the American ways.

I can easily understand how hard it is for Japanese who return home to write to America. One has so little time for doing anything. People do not seem to regard the hours and are never in a hurry, or do things promptly, and they do seem to take a long time to do anything at all.

Now I have one astonishing piece of news to tell you which took my breath away when I heard it. Shige is to be married on the first of December! The day the steamer sails with this letter she will be Mrs. Uriu. So often as Sutematsu and I have talked about it we never dreamed of anything like this. It is rather sudden. You see, next year Mr. Uriu[8] will be ordered away, and they want to be married a little while before he goes, and so they settled it between them. She will be married at his home according to custom, with a foreign service read in Japanese by a Japanese minister. . . . They will begin housekeeping immediately by themselves and live in partially foreign style. Is it not

---

7   Umeko's sister, older by two years. Also called Kotoko.

8   Uriu Sotokichi (1857–1937) was a navy officer who later became a rear admiral of the Imperial Navy.

surprising? Sutematsu and I don't want Shige married first thing, but we can't help it. I am worried to know what to give her for a present.

. . .

You know, on the steamer every one of the officers teased me so much about my smallness of size. They always made some remark, and told me many things about little people. But now in Japan I feel so big. Shige and all who knew me in America say I have grown. There is not one whit difference in height between Koto and myself and my mother is one inch taller. I am catching up to Shige. Sutematsu is uncomfortably tall for Japan. What a land of little people it is anyway!

. . .

I have not seen enough to express my opinion of the country and of my impression, but though many things come back to me, still it does not seem natural at all. I still feel in a dream and would not be surprised at awakening. I feel constantly as if I was not to stay but more as if I were visiting.

Do not worry about me, dear Mrs. Lanman. I am in such a happy home and with kind friends, and so though I may find it hard to get accustomed to many things and often feel strange and lonely, I have so many blessings and so many friends that come to see me, and who I will know better by and by, that soon I shall feel that this is my own true home and America only a preparing place. I long to be able to speak and begin working, and I think the language will come easily. The words I learn I put in constant use and hear all the time and so I must learn soon. Koto helps me and interprets for me, and teaches me how to say some common phrases and Japanese is an easy language. Oh, I don't want to lose my English as Shige has. She has sometimes difficulty in expressing herself fully, and some words that are not in common use, she forgets. I must read and write and talk and keep it up.

. . . To everybody that comes we offer tea and cake or oranges and they take some, so when I go around, I have to drink lots of tea and eat candy or something always, for even if you don't want it, you must take it, though you leave it untasted.

Tomorrow, Koto says, I must make some calls and so I, in my turn, carry fish or fruit or something. When I go with so many calls it is, and must always be, dreadfully inconvenient. But such is the custom and it is unchangeable. . . .

In spite of my bringing up and my long stay of ten years in America and my American ways entirely, it is not one half as strange or as hard for me to do Japanese ways as for an American, so you see we[9] are more Japanese than people give us credit for, and someday, if ever I return to America, your ways may seem difficult. . . .

You would be astonished to see with what curiosity everything of mine is regarded. My dresses have been shown over and over again—all my various things, hats, ribbons and everything. You would have been astonished to see the regular show here one afternoon. I have given away some hairpins as curiosities, and the things I have given away are considered so curious.

. . . In a word, everything American is regarded with the same curiosity as Japanese things in America—and it seems strange to me, who have come so soon from one country to the other in so short a space of time.

. . . I feel so strange, like a tree that is transplanted and takes a little while to get accustomed to new surroundings. And think to what different soil I have been transplanted. And then too I shall be puzzled so often to know what to do. How much to keep of American ways,

---

9   Umeko refers to Sutematsu, Shige, and herself. Her use of "we" seems to indicate that she always thinks of the three as being set apart from other Japanese.

and how much to go back, and so often I wonder how I am going to do any good to my country-women, and how I must begin. The way is dark and dreary. I hope your prayers will go up with mine for guidance in this tangled maze.

Small things, such as the way Japanese people stood and sat a hundred years ago, still live on in the way people conduct themselves today. Returnees from abroad have become commonplace in Japan, but they only serve to emphasize the habits that flow on unchanged beneath the upheavals of the past century.

Reading Umeko's letters, I am reminded of how I too left Japan more than two decades ago, around the time that Japanese people finally began to stop talking about living in the "postwar" era. I lived in America for eleven years and returned to Japan in the middle of the great economic boom era. I remember how people looked me over from head to toe with a mixture of envy and scorn, and responded to a chance remark of mine with a "Well, she was in America" look and a knowing smirk.

. . . My father was talking the other day about the money spent on me and said that it would have been enough in Japan to support a family more than comfortably, and he added the nation paid it for me and I must work hard to return the obligation. Sutematsu and I think that even if no obstacle offers itself, and all is made easy for us to return to America, even in many years, a moral obligation would make us stay in Japan and treat it as our home. Of course this obligation would not exclude a visit to America and to this I must look forward. . . .

The government had paid a thousand dollars per annum for the girls' tuition, and also granted them a liberal traveling allowance. In those days, the exchange rate for the dollar seems to have fluctuated between one and two yen. To offer a few figures in comparison: in 1880, a day laborer might earn twenty-one sen [= 0.21 yen] per diem; in 1886, the starting monthly salary for an elementary school teacher was five yen; in 1894, a civil servant was paid fifty yen per month. In 1878, annual tuition for a prefectural middle school was nine yen, and in 1879, annual tuition for Tokyo Imperial University was twelve yen.[10]

A thousand dollars per annum between 1871 and 1882 indeed seems sufficient to have kept a family in comfort. The young Umeko's touchingly stubborn sense of patriotism reflected circumstances that prevailed eleven years earlier, when people came upon the idea of dispatching five young girls to a foreign land and keeping them there at the cost of the nation.

About three years ago—it was the summer of 1986, I think—Kawazu Sanae, an editor of Asahi Shimbun's publishing division, paid me a visit. She began to tell me about the discovery in an old storage room of a hoard of letters written by Tsuda Umeko, founder of Tsuda College, addressed to a Mrs. Adeline Lanman. Kawazu said that the correspondence was valuable material that shed light on the innermost thoughts of the founder as a young woman, who lived and studied abroad for a decade and returned to Japan during the exhilarating Rokumeikan years. She suggested that I, as an alumna of Tsuda College, was just the person to take a fresh look at Umeko's words and weave a story out of them.

Actually, I had already heard something about these letters from

---

10 *Nedan no Meiji, Taishō, Shōwa fūzoku-shi* [History of Prices in the Meiji, Taishō, and Shōwa Eras], ed. Shūkan Asahi (Tokyo: Asahi Shimbunsha, 1981-82). The figures are taken from various tables scattered throughout the three volumes.

Sakagami Masayuki, an administrator at Tsuda College, and assumed that the school would not make them public until they had a better idea of their content. But if, indeed, the school was thinking of permitting an outsider to read them, my writer's soul jumped at the chance of being that person.

I had written several short essays about Tsuda Umeko as a representative woman of the Meiji era and knew something of her writings, but most of the materials I had read were written in her official capacity as founder of Joshi Eigaku Juku (Women's School for English Studies, precursor of Tsuda College). I began to dream of a vibrant Tsuda Umeko who would come to life in the newly discovered letters. So Kawazu made numerous visits to the college and brought me the letters as they were progressively transcribed on a word-processor, and before I knew it, I was deep in Umeko's world.

It was like viewing a sepia-colored motion picture of an early modern Japan not found in the history books, revealing the inner workings of Meiji society and the figures and souls of the people who lived in it—portraits of a world seen through the eyes of the woman Umeko. I could see living people sitting or standing in the scenes she described, and there was Umeko, too, watching them, biting her lip.

In February 1984, the letters had been found slumbering in a storeroom on the rooftop of a turret-like structure nicknamed the Tower, perched above the third floor of Tsuda College's main building. A student noticed a few letters that had fallen out of an old trunk and notified school authorities.

The discovery caused something of an uproar at the school. Why were the letters there? To this day, no one really knows. Why had hundreds of private letters written by Umeko to Adeline Lanman between 1882 and 1911, as well as approximately one hundred letters written by Adeline to Umeko, been abandoned together in this place?

After caring for Umeko for eleven years, Adeline Lanman sent her home in 1882 with a neatly sorted bundle of Umeko's own writing and any letters she had received from Japan. These documents proved valuable years later when biographies of Umeko were undertaken. For example, Japanese writings by the very young Umeko and letters from her mother Hatsuko were cited in both Yoshikawa Toshikazu's *Tsuda Umeko den* (A Biography of Tsuda Umeko)[11] and Yamazaki Takako's *Tsuda Umeko*[12] and informed some of the books' most memorable passages.

It is likely that Adeline Lanman returned Umeko's letters to her sometime before her own death in 1914. The last letter is dated 1911, only a few years before Adeline's death. Umeko saw Adeline in 1913 when she traveled to the United States to attend a meeting of the World Student Christian Federation as a delegate for the Japanese YWCA. Adeline was eighty-seven years old and growing frail in both body and mind. Umeko took care of matters concerning her house and looked after Adeline personally, so it is possible that she received the letters at that time.

In any case, judging from the fact that Umeko's and Adeline's letters were found together, it would seem that either Umeko herself, or someone very close to her and interested in her life story, received them from the original owners and placed them together. There is a strong likelihood that this "someone" was Anna Hartshorne, an intimate friend and helpmate of Umeko, who also taught for many years at the school. Hirata Yasuko, who took part in organizing and editing the correspondence, says this theory is supported by a number of comments jotted on the letters, probably by Hartshorne.

Umeko passed away in 1929, but Anna Hartshorne devoted herself to the school for many years afterward and remained in Japan until the eve of World War II in 1940, when she went home for what she intended to be a short visit. It is very likely that she hoped to write a posthumous biography

---

11 Yoshikawa Toshikazu, *Tsuda Umeko den* [Biography of Tsuda Umeko], rev. ed. Tokyo: Tsuda Juku Dōsōkai, 1956 (first published 1930).

12 Yamazaki Takako, *Tsuda Umeko*, new ed. Tokyo: Yoshikawa Kōbunkan, 1988 (first published 1962).

of Umeko, or have one written, for there are signs that she had begun to sort the letters, as well as other documents. The things she left behind in her apartment on campus when she departed in 1940 were probably moved to the storeroom together with her other belongings. Anna Hartshorne passed away in 1957 without stepping on Japanese soil again. And the letters remained where they were, forgotten. When Yoshikawa Toshikazu compiled his *Tsuda Umeko den*, he cited portions of the earlier mentioned letters written by Umeko when she was very young, but made no mention of any letters to Adeline Lanman.

It is entirely possible that Umeko gave them to Anna Hartshorne instead of throwing them out. Hirata says there are signs that Umeko reread some of them herself. She must have thought that it would be permissible for them to be made public at some time or other, after her own death. The letters are full of genuine feelings that sometimes verge on cries of anguish or anger, meant only for the eyes of her foster mother.

As for myself, I am taken back to 1949, when I became a student at Tsuda College in the spring of my eighteenth year. I was roughly the same age as Umeko when she returned to Japan after eleven years of life and study abroad. I was born and raised in Tokyo, but my family lived in my mother's home prefecture of Niigata during the years after the war. When I returned to Tokyo from there, I was horrified to see the city reduced to an endless expanse of burnt rubble. Shacks were going up here and there, but food was still in short supply, and Ueno Station, where the trains from Niigata arrived, swarmed with war orphans.

My primary reason for choosing Tsuda College was its dormitory, which accepted all applicants. No parent would willingly send a child to the ruins of Tokyo without a reasonable prospect of lodgings and food. I think about 90 percent of the four hundred or so students at the college boarded there. The food depended on the students' ration cards, but the school provided us with a place to sleep and eat, which was a rare blessing in those days.

Kodaira, where the Tsuda campus is located, is presently a residential suburb of Tokyo, but back then, there were only a few scattered houses in the area. The school had a cozy, secluded atmosphere, with buildings playing hide-and-seek among the trees of the Musashino woods.

After an hour-long train ride on the Chūō line from Tokyo station to Kokubunji, the burnt-out cityscape gave way to woodland, forest, and tree-lined roads. At Kokubunji, I changed to a train on a private line that ran only once an hour, and got off at a lonely little station named "Takanodai" (Hawk's Perch) that looked exactly like the kind of place a hawk would perch on a high branch to survey the land. All around were woods and mulberry fields, and the people walking among the trees were mostly Tsuda students. It struck me as too lonely a place for a young woman to be.

The dormitory was located right on campus, within sight of the main college building, with a pine thicket and lawn in between. There was a stand of cherry trees nearby, as well as plum trees, chestnuts, and a bamboo thicket. The cherry blossoms were in full bloom on the day I arrived at the dormitory. I sat down underneath one of the trees and idly thought about life at the school for the next four years and about the life that was supposedly waiting for me beyond that.

Cherry blossoms at their peak bring to mind the angst of young adulthood. I looked up to see a glimpse of blue sky through the thick layers of blossoms. The almost overpowering scent of the flowers and the moist, delicate texture of the fine petals reminded me how easily they would be scattered and trampled by the next day. I remember with strange clarity that moment

Ōba Minako on the campus of Tsuda College. (1950)

of agitation, mixed with an inexplicable foreboding, as I sat under the cherry tree. The memory makes me sentimental about what it is to be young.

While sitting under the tree, I made the acquaintance of an old woman who resembled a flower sprite. Thinking back, I realize that she was probably somewhere between fifty and sixty years old, but to a young girl of eighteen, she seemed like a very old lady. She was apparently an alumna of Tsuda who had come to the school on an errand. Like me, she had stopped under the tree to look up at the flowers in their glory, and when she noticed that I was a new student, she began to talk to me in a rambling way. "You know, Tsuda-sensei did research on frogs' eggs. At a college in America."

I knew no such thing about Tsuda Umeko and stared at her blankly. I knew that Tsuda College had once been called the Women's School for English Studies and that its students were known for their proficiency in English, so I more or less assumed that its founder, Tsuda Umeko, had studied English literature or linguistics. Knowing next to nothing about Umeko, I had taken a liking to the school on the basis of a subjective impression of a small college with a personal feel to it. But research on frogs' eggs? I stared at the woman in surprise. She went on.

"You know about the anarchist Ōsugi Sakae, don't you? The one who was killed in the Taishō era together with Itō Noe? Ōsugi was already stabbed once before by another lover of his, Kamichika Ichiko, because of a complicated love triangle involving three, or perhaps four, people. Kamichika Ichiko—the one who stabbed Ōsugi—was a classmate of mine. But it was such a dishonorable affair that the school erased her name from the list of alumnae."

She looked up at the cherry blossoms and sighed deeply.

"Why do they go on blooming, year after year? And frogs keep being born."

It seemed to me that the woman had a northern accent. She began to talk again about someone named Hatano Akiko, who committed double suicide with the novelist Arishima Takeo.[13] Akiko was a married woman and adultery was a criminal offense back then (1923), so the couple could not stay together despite their mutual love. So they hanged themselves in Arishima's villa in Karuizawa.

"Hatano Akiko wasn't a Tsuda graduate, but she was here for a while. Akiko was *so* particular about her appearance. She used to say that she indulged in dressing up because she was so unhappy. Now, I wonder what she meant."

She spoke as if she had known Akiko personally.

"When Akiko died, Itō Noe disparaged her and said she wasn't in the least bit intellectual. I think there was a touch of envy there. Either that, or they were too much alike in temperament. It was only a few months after Takeo and Akiko committed suicide that Itō Noe and Ōsugi Sakae were killed together."

The woman gazed up again at the flowers, looked hard at the eighteen-year-old me, then shook her head as if overcome by sentiment.

"The same flowers bloom year after year, but the people you meet are always different, they say. But when I see a young person like yourself, I do think that people are also like flowers. Both people and flowers bloom and scatter, and they drop little seeds. Tsuda-sensei studied frogs' eggs, you see."

"Yes, that's how it is," she said.

She shook her head again and pointed beyond the cherry trees, saying:

"Tsuda-sensei's grave is over there."

I thought about the feminist activist Kamichika Ichiko,[14] who was still living, and about the people who died strange deaths during the Taishō era. I also thought about the older students who had passed me in the

---

13 Arishima Takeo (1878–1923) was a well-known writer and intellectual leader of the late Meiji through Taishō eras.

14 Kamichika Ichiko (1888–1981) was a prolific writer, critic, and politician who served as a member of the House of Representatives for a time.

dormitory speaking in upper-class jargon, and the students my own age with decidedly unchic hairdos who looked like they never did anything but study. I felt some trepidation, but also an odd wave of rising excitement, as I looked toward the grave that the woman was pointing at.

"In those days, there was something about the school that drew young Japanese women who were awakening to themselves. Women who were beginning to think about their place in the world had the feeling that they would find something here, at the Women's School for English Studies."

"Is it still so?" I asked timidly.

"Who knows? I rather think that America-philes come here these days. I suppose that is something else we should be thinking about."

The woman, who wore a drab kimono, spoke somewhat angrily.

"Tsuda-sensei always dressed Japanese-style."

I wonder why I have always remembered that conversation.

Recently I checked a Tsuda alumnae register and found the name Kamichika Ichiko. I could not find Hatano Akiko, not even in the list of affiliates, but Miyata Marie, an editor at the publisher Chūō Kōronsha, where Akiko also worked as an editor, kindly provided me with reference material from Akiko's time. The July 10, 1923 edition of the *Osaka Mainichi Shimbun* reported the love-pact suicide, stating: "Akiko attended the Women's School for English Studies in Kojimachi after her marriage."

Be that as it may, I wonder who she was—that woman I met under the cherry tree?

It is true that Tsuda Umeko majored in biology at Bryn Mawr College. In 1894, she co-authored a paper on frogs' eggs with T.H. Morgan, and their paper was published in the British *Journal of Microscopical Science*. In 1933, T.H. Morgan was awarded the Nobel Prize for his work in genetics. Years later, he praised Umeko's aptitude and character, saying that she had a fine mind but had given up biology altogether in order to become an educator.

2
DREAMS

**Monday
November 27, 1882**

Today ends my first week in Japan. A strange week of strange experiences and yet withal a pleasant week. The last two days have been quite eventful. Father wrote to Mr. Kuroda[1] asking when I could call and pay my respects and he answered and settled [on] Saturday, so on that morning I got into a jinricksha and called for Sutematsu. She lives five miles away, a long distance. When I reached her home I asked her to go with me and she consented and dressed in her American dress, for, you see, she was in Japanese clothes. When she came back she took lunch and went to Mr. Kuroda's near here. He received us in a foreign room with Father as interpreter. A fine distinguished soldier-like man he was, and he conversed with us in the Japanese-style, expressing many compliments about our education and rather embarrassing us, but we managed to thank him. He then asked us to stay and hear some blind musicians on *koto* and *samisen*, the best in Tokio. So we stayed, and he entertained us and we had refreshments and heard some queer music, but very fine according to their ideas. Then geishas sang. All this was for our benefit and we may say we were royally treated. There were other gentlemen present besides Mrs. Kuroda and attendants. Finally Mr. Kuroda asked us to sing a song in English and as we could not refuse, and no one

---

1   Japanese politician Kuroda Kiyotaka (1840–1900), vice-chairman of the Hokkaido Development Commission (Kaitakushi), had visions of educating women and was instrumental in sending Umeko to study in America. The Commission provided the funds for her tuition and that of the other girls. The "Mr. Kuroda" in Umeko's letter is no doubt this man, although he was no longer in control of the Commission after 1881.

who knew music was present, Sutematsu and I dragged through "In the Gloaming" and "Jesus, Lover of my Soul"—a thing I never did before, and want to laugh at the idea of it even now. We stayed at Mr. Kuroda's three hours altogether. As it was so late, I made Sutematsu stay all night and she and I had such a nice talk about our work, and decided we were in a hard position, harder by far than missionaries who can say out and out what they want. All these great men in Japan are not Christians and are, besides, very immoral. We feel that we are only a drop in the sea. Next day, yesterday, was Sunday, so we went to Union Church with Shige and heard the services in English, and I met some of the missionaries. I enjoyed the service very much. On our return home Koto took me to see Aunt who is an attendant in the palace of Prince Tokugawa. He has been in England five years and only came back a steamer or two before me. He does not live in the home near here, but his mother does, and he came yesterday to see her and Aunt wanted me to see him in this way. Ordinarily his rank is too high for him to see such as I. In fact, before the revolution, Koto says, he was as high as Mikado, but not so now.

He talked to me in English and I conversed quite freely considering the distance in rank. He spoke of his journey and I told of mine. He is quite pleasant and said he sympathized with me in sitting down on floors. Besides his conversation, my visit was dreadfully tiresome. So many attendants chatting in Japanese, and I not saying a word, and for their benefit I took off my hat and showed it, stood up, and turned around for them to look at my dress and buttons, my bangles and everything on me, from my hair down.

These excerpts from Umeko's letters are transcribed from her handwriting, which is old-fashioned and not always easy to decipher. Moreover, she had only recently returned home and was hearing unfamiliar Japanese terms that she spelled out as well as she could in Roman letters, and describing things as she imagined them to be without background knowledge of Japan.

At the beginning of this letter, she mentions a visit to Kuroda Kiyotaka (1840–1900) with her father, Tsuda Sen (1837–1908), who acted as interpreter. Both Kiyotaka and Sen are people who stir my imagination. Kuroda Kiyotaka was an influential member of the Hokkaido Development Commission, which provided the funds to send Umeko and the other girls to America. He was a native of the Satsuma domain and one of its elders, and as such, was often at odds with the statesman Itō Hirobumi (1841–1909), who was a native of Chōshū.[2] In 1888, after Itō dissolved his cabinet and resigned as prime minister, Kuroda took over the position but resigned after only a year and a half. He held various high posts afterwards and is famous for rehabilitating Enomoto Takeaki, who fought against him in the Battle of Goryōkaku,[3] and subsequently appointing him to an important position. Kuroda was reputedly a man who could think in international terms, and this can be seen in his leadership of the Commission and in his handling of matters relating to Karafuto (Sakhalin).[4] Guided by the concept that education is the driving force of development, he laid the groundwork for Sapporo Agricultural College (precursor of Hokkaido University) and

2   The domains of Satsuma and Chōshū had a long history of enmity, but joined in an uneasy alliance to overthrow the Edo shogunate and restore the emperor. This was the prelude to the Meiji Restoration and the democratization and modernization that followed.

3   Fort Goryōkaku in Hakodate was the site of the final battle between the Tokugawa shogunate's army and imperial troops (composed primarily of samurai from the Chōshū and Satsuma domains). It took place from October 1868 to May 1869 and is also referred to as the Battle of Hakodate. Enomoto Takeaki (1836–1908) fought for the shogunate, but Kuroda's patronage permitted him to rise again and he became one of the founders of the Imperial Japanese Navy.

4   The sparsely populated island of Sakhalin, inhabited primarily by indigenous tribes, has long been the source of a power struggle between Japan and Russia / Soviet Union for the sake of its gas and oil resources. Both countries attempted to colonize the island in the nineteenth century, with Russians presiding over the north and Japanese the southern part of the island. The Soviet Union took control of the island in 1945 when it seized the Japanese portion at the end of World War II.

adopted the American frontier spirit as one of its leading principles. He was also greatly interested in women's education, based on the idea that a country's future depends upon the resourcefulness of its mothers.

In 1871, Kuroda went to America to observe its development projects and was extremely impressed at the high status of women in that country. He spoke with Mori Arinori (1847–1889), who was stationed in America at the time as a chargé d'affaires,[5] and reportedly told Mori that the quickest way to reform Japan was for Japanese people to marry Americans, and that since he (Mori) was still single, he ought to take an American wife.

Beginning with the rehabilitation of Enomoto Takeaki, Kuroda was able to assemble a capable team of old shogunate hands with knowhow about international affairs. His far-sightedness is well reflected in the Hokkaido Development Commission's recruitment of young girls to send to America.

The five girls who applied were as follows:

Yoshimasu Ryōko, fifteen, born to a former samurai family of Tokyo; daughter of Yoshimasu Masao, a civil officer of Akita prefecture.

Ueda Teiko, fifteen, daughter of Ueda Shun, a low ranking official of the foreign ministry.

Yamakawa Sutematsu, twelve, born to a former samurai family of Aomori; younger sister of Yamakawa Yoshichirō (also called Hiroshi).

Nagai Shigeko, nine, born to a former samurai family of Shizuoka; daughter of Nagai Kyūtarō.

Tsuda Umeko, eight, born to a former samurai family of Tokyo; daughter of Tsuda Sen.[6]

5　Diplomat who heads an embassy in the absence of the ambassador.

6　Ages are given here according to the traditional method of counting age in Japan, whereby people are one year old at birth and add another year every New Year's Day. This makes them one or two years older than by the modern count.

A quick glance at the list reveals that the girls were not particularly close to the new Meiji government. They tended rather to be offspring of factions of the old samurai class who had had their eyes on the West from early on. Umeko's father, Tsuda Sen, was born to a family of retainers of the Sakura domain. He was later adopted into the Tsuda clan, who were treasurers for the shogunate. He married Tsuda Hatsuko and Umeko was their second daughter.

Sen studied Dutch and English as a young man and became a magistrate of foreign affairs for the shogunate. He also held a position in the Niigata magisterial office, and worked for a time at the Tsukiji Hotel in Tokyo[7] after the Meiji Restoration. Later, he established a farm in the Azabu district of Tokyo where he grew Western-style vegetables. He also founded a school of agriculture named Gakunōsha[8] and launched *Nōgyō zasshi*, an agricultural magazine that explained modern farming methods. He had accompanied Fukuzawa Yukichi[9] on his American tour during the final years of the shogunate, attended the Vienna World's Fair after the new imperial government was established, and came home with dreams of improving and modernizing Japanese agriculture.

Nōgyō zasshi had a circulation of three or four thousand to more than ten thousand at one time, and attracted a large nationwide readership among people interested in new agricultural methods. Sen introduced new techniques and invented a number of agricultural devices including the "Tsuda rope," a twisted rope used to aid pollination.

---

7 The Tsukiji Hotel opened in the first year of Meiji (1868) and was Japan's first Western-style hotel.

8 Iwamoto Yoshiharu, later founder and editor of *Jogaku zasshi*, a women's studies journal that introduced writers such as Kitamura Tōkoku and Shimazaki Tōson to the literary world, was an alumnus of Gakunōsha.

9 Fukuzawa Yukichi (1835–1901) was an eminent writer, educator, and entrepreneur who founded Keio University.

Sen's Gakunōsha predated the founding of Sapporo Agricultural College by six months and his innovative spirit swept the nation like a wind of reform. During his trip to the United States in 1867, he had no one to dress his hair and so became one of the first men of the samurai class to cut off his topknot. When the Meiji era began, he ordered his wife Hatsuko to stop blackening her teeth (the traditional sign of a married woman) and shaving her eyebrows, which gave her an unusual and revolutionary look. No doubt the decision to send their young daughter to America was another of his eccentric ideas.

When Sen returned from America without his topknot, the neighbors felt sorry for his wife and whispered among themselves: "How she must suffer—the poor, poor lady—to have her husband come home in such a state!" When he saw his young daughter off from the port of Yokohama, they reportedly said: "What a bizarre way for parents to behave. To send such a little girl off to America, which might as well be the end of the world. The father is what he is, but the mother must have the heart of an ogre to agree to such a thing!"[10] And so went the gossip, but the fact is that Tsuda Sen and Kuroda Kiyotaka were two men with great visions of what the girls might accomplish.

Let me mention in passing that Kuroda, who advised Mori Arinori to take an American wife, was rumored in 1878—while the girls were in America—to have killed his wife, Sei. Kuroda tended to drunken rages, and rumor said that he either killed his young wife (who was more than ten years his junior) with a sword or beat her to death. *Marumaru chinbun*, a weekly satire magazine, came out with a full-page cartoon accompanied by a sardonic but humorous exposé of the affair.

---

10 Yamazaki, *Tsuda Umeko*, 21, 43.

Historian Irokawa Daikichi recounts the affair as follows:

... You can't put the lid on spreading rumor. Kuroda finally handed in his resignation and hid away in his house.

According to a memo by Chisaka Takamasa, secretary to Iwakura (Tomomi), Itō (Hirobumi) and Ōkuma (Shigenobu) insisted that the culprit be punished, as Japan is a nation ruled by law. Home Minister Ōkubo (Toshimichi), finding himself in a corner, declared: "Kuroda is not a cold-blooded monster who would do such a thing. I guarantee this and ask you to leave the matter to me for a while."

So he said and ordered Kawaji Toshiyoshi, head of the police department, to conduct an autopsy. So Kawaji, in the company of a handful of underlings and a doctor, had the grave opened. He approached the coffin, peered inside, looked around, and declared: "There is no evidence of murder." Everyone else was silent.

And so the "official procedure" came to an end, and Kuroda was persuaded by Ōkubo to withdraw his letter of resignation.[11]

A few days later, Ōkubo was attacked and killed at Kioizaka by Shimada Ichirō and other former samurai from Ishikawa prefecture. The assasins' written statement was as follows.

Here we declare those who deserve death. The chief scoundrels are Kido Takayoshi, Ōkubo Toshimichi, and Iwakura Tomomi. Ōkuma Shigenobu, Itō Hirobumi, Kuroda Kiyotaka and Kawaji Toshiyoshi are also not to be forgiven. . . . When the roots are severed, the branches and leaves will wither and fall.[12]

---

11 Irokawa Daikichi, *Nihon no rekishi 21: Kindai kokka no shuppatsu* [History of Japan vol. 21: Beginning of the Modern State] (Tokyo: Chūō Kōronsha, 1974/2006), 24-25.

12 Ibid., 26.

The event that triggered the assassination may well have been Ōkubo's shielding of Kuroda in the matter of his wife's death. Kuroda himself was unscathed and eventually became a prime minister of Japan.

On the other hand, some people categorically deny that there was anything untoward about the wife's death. In his book *Kuroda Kiyotaka* (1977),[13] Iguro Yatarō asserts that Sei had tuberculosis and that her death was a result of hemoptysis. He suggests that the rumors were spread by sympathizers of Saigō Takamori after Saigō's death in the Satsuma Rebellion, because they were angry that Kuroda refused to martyr himself alongside Saigō. The rumors were entirely without foundation, he writes, and adds that Kuroda adopted Sei's younger sister Hyakuko and that Hyakuko in her old age reminisced pleasantly about Kuroda and Sei together, and that while most powerful men of the day eagerly took on a mistress or two, Kuroda steadfastly cherished his invalid wife until her death. Judging from these facts, it is inconceivable that he killed her, he concludes. Fukuzawa Yukichi also wrote an essay in *Minkan zasshi* (People's Magazine) denying the rumors, and it is really no longer possible to verify the truth one way or the other.

In any case, Umeko's visit to Kuroda took place in late November 1882, a year after a scandal regarding the sale of Hokkaido Development Commission assets triggered a political crisis involving Kuroda as well as Ōkuma Shigenobu, Itō Hirobumi, Fukuzawa Yukichi, Iwasaki Yatarō, Inoue Kaoru, and others. The root of the crisis was a sale orchestrated by Kuroda of various public assets. He appears to have been keeping a low profile during the following year, disgruntled but silent. It must have given him profound satisfaction to meet the young women at this period of his life. After all, they were the little girls he had sent abroad eleven years earlier, when his own dreams were young and unsullied.

---

13 Iguro Yatarō, *Kuroda Kiyotaka* (Tokyo: Yoshikawa Kōbunkan, 1977/1987), 117-19.

Whether Kuroda's wife died by her husband's hand or from illness, I cannot help feeling that the wife who died so young and the dreams he invested in the girls he sent abroad were somehow linked in his mind.

When Kuroda encouraged Mori Arinori to take an American wife, he himself was already married. I wonder if he looked at his young wife (who some say was only thirteen years old at the time of their marriage, although others say she was sixteen) and had visions of Japanese wives someday being as grand as the women he met in American society, well-educated and capable of holding their own with menfolk. Perhaps he despaired of the Japanese women who were his reality and was unhappy that he and other men had moulded them to be that way over the long course of Japanese history.

Kuroda's treatment of the women in his day-to-day life, and of his wife, was on a different level from his vision of Japan's women of the future. His impatience with the gap between dream and reality must have created a great tangle in his mind that rose to the surface when he was drunk, as he was wont to be, so there was fertile ground for people to think of him as the kind of man who might murder his wife.

The world we live in is not really made up so much of facts, but of what people think the facts are. After all, why do people read novels? Why does literature not die out? There are things that cannot be said out loud, but which people contemplate in their minds, and they like to know that there are other people who share those thoughts. And sometimes, at some point in time and space, such dreams and imaginings lead to real actions.

Wherever the truth lay, Kuroda was beleaguered by rumors surrounding his wife's death. And a few years before that, he had made the decision to send a group of young girls, as young or younger than his youthful wife, to live and study in a foreign land. In the ten years that followed, his wife Sei died a suspicious death and his state of mind may have undergone a complete change. It is hard to know what his thoughts were when Yamakawa Sutematsu and Tsuda Umeko stood before him.

Umeko writes of Kuroda that "he conversed with us in the Japanese-style, expressing many compliments about our education." Her impressions of the refreshments and entertainment offered at Kuroda's home contain a hint not only of perplexity, but a measure of discomfort with the whole situation. She mentions that Mrs. Kuroda was also present, but this would be the woman he married after Sei.

> . . . [we] decided we were in a hard position, harder by far than missionaries who can say out and out what they want. All these great men in Japan are not Christians and are, besides, very immoral. We feel that we are only a drop in the ocean.

What were the thoughts behind these words? Was Umeko aware of the suspicions surrounding the death of Kuroda's wife a few years before? Did she know about the political crisis that followed? About the scandal involving the sale of public assets in Hokkaido? Perusing her letters, the reader is free to imagine how Japan unfolded before Umeko's eyes in the week after her return home.

Umeko's father grew Western-style vegetables on his farm in Azabu and provided Western-style meals for the daughter who had come home from America. He also prepared what he considered to be Western-style furniture for her use and acted as her interpreter. As the founder of Gakunōsha, he had worked with the Hokkaido Development Commission and knew Kuroda Kiyotaka better than most people.

"Prince Tokugawa" probably refers to Tokugawa Iesato (1863–1940). Iesato's mother Takeko was the elder sister of Umeko's mother Hatsuko. Takeko was a lady-in-waiting in the household of Yoshiyori, a member of the Tayasu branch of the Tokugawa family. She gave birth to two boys, Iesato and Satotaka, but it is unclear if Umeko was aware of this private family matter. Umeko's elder sister Koto did not speak English well enough to translate in detail, and even if she had been able to do so, it is doubtful that she would have told her sister, who had just returned from abroad, about the connection between Iesato and Takeko, who was, after all, only a concubine. Or it could be that Umeko was perfectly aware of the situation, but refrained from mentioning it to Adeline.

In her letter, she speaks of "Aunt," "Prince Tokugawa," and "his mother," but we can only guess at how much she actually knew. Iesato became the head of the Tokugawa family after Yoshinobu[14] was ousted by the Meiji government and forced into retirement, so Umeko's expression "before the revolution . . . he was as high as Mikado" no doubt means that he would have been the shogun in an earlier age.[15]

Iesato studied in England from 1877 to 1882 and returned to Japan only shortly before Umeko, which was probably why the meeting was arranged. Years later, in 1931, after Umeko's death, Iesato was a guest of honor at the dedication ceremony for a new school building on Tsuda College's Kodaira campus. There, he gave a congratulatory speech in English that honored Umeko, founder of the school, as a woman before her time and a groundbreaking educator of the women who would build the future.

Wednesday
November 29, 1882

. . . Shige will be married day after tomorrow. . . . Sutematsu and I hate to have Shige married . . . but of course, we don't say anything. She

---

14 Tokugawa Yoshinobu (1837-1913) was the 15th and last Tokugawa shogun. He succeeded to the position in 1866 in a time of great political turmoil and was forced to tender his resignation to the emperor a year later, after the shogunate itself was overthrown.

15 "Mikado" refers to the emperor, whereas the head of the Tokugawa family was the shogun, whose status theoretically was that of a retainer appointed by the emperor.

will be married very very quietly, only ourselves and Shige's family present.

. . .

To be sure I often think of America with affection, and hope some day to revisit it, but still I am Japanese and must stay here. I think of you very often and nothing will ever make me forget my old home, associations, and old haunts, and all your loving kindness. Whatever comes I shall always have these pleasant recollections and you in American to think of.

My Father, too, is very kind and indulgent, but seems to expect far too much from his foreign daughter. He introduces me to people, I think with a proud way and already wants and asks me to do many things which I don't know. I hope his anticipation in me will not be too suddenly overthrown.

Early December[16]

. . . I am expecting my boxes soon, and shall hail the arrival of the piano with delight.

Next Sunday at a native service Mr. Kozaki the minister wanted me to play on piano for the singing. I am going to try, though I may not know the hymns. But it is better to get accustomed and then there is no one else to play.

I help my father with his writing, and already have written several letters some of them on business. I wish however that his letter and everything were a little more systematic. Procrastination too is a national defect.

. . .

---

16 This letter is not clearly dated, but it was sent with the one dated November 29.

I wish I could give you a taste of the *kakis* that are in their season. They are delicious and I never tire of them, and Japanese candies, too. Japanese food is very nice and it has agreed with me very well indeed. It is strange how natural everything tastes. Oh, if the language would only come back to me as easily! I am bound hand and foot, I am both deaf and dumb. My father promises to get me some instruction books, but has not yet, and I have learned but little, sad to say, though Koto tries to teach me. But when there are six or seven ways to say anything and they tell me all, I get in a muddle truly. Everywhere I go I must have some one as interpreter. I can't go about, walk, shop, visit, even take a jinricksha ride alone. Then I don't know the city at all, such a big place as it is, so here I am idling away the precious hours and not learning much and doing but so little.

It was only a week since her return and Umeko was growing impatient and beset by anxiety and despair. The culture shock of new feelings and experiences made the time seem long to her and she suddenly felt older than she was. She had been to Nagai Shigeko's wedding and was disheartened that her friend should forsake her mission as a government-sponsored student and marry. After the wedding, Umeko asked Sutematsu to stay overnight at her home in Azabu and they talked again about the difficulties they faced.

Sutematsu and Umeko were perplexed that the Ministry of Education was showing no interest in them after expending public money to keep them in America for ten years. They wondered what they had studied so hard for and were beginning to worry if they would ever be given any work. Men who went abroad to study came home and were given suitable positions in which they could utilize the knowledge they brought back to the benefit of their country. Apparently, there were no suitable jobs for women, simply because they were women.

In addition, so many things they heard and saw in Japan were not at all pleasant. For example, Tsukiji in those days was a special quarter set aside for foreigners, but Umeko was distinctly displeased by the foreign missionaries who lived there.

> They call these great minds heathen, half civilized and etc. And then they are apt to force matters, and as Shige says they meet a gentleman—"You are Mr. Masuda. Yes. You are not a Christian, now why are you not?"[17]

After writing this, Umeko added that these were secret thoughts and that it would cause trouble if it came out that she thought that way. She was upset with Americans in Japan, and at the same time, she was also impatient with Japanese who had been to America. For example, when Japanese went to America and returned home, they wrote few letters and the customs of their land made them slow in doing anything, she explained. She was constantly offering excuses for their behavior, worried that Adeline would think badly of them. Even Umeko's father, Sen, was always saying that he must write to the Lanmans and thank them for taking care of Umeko during her long stay, but he was slow in getting the job done. Please don't think he is ungrateful because the thank you letter is slow in coming, Umeko wrote.

So Umeko was vexed with people, and the incomprehensible customs of the Japanese were causing her acute embarrassment or shock, one after the other.

> . . . then in the streets everywhere, are the buildings for the men to go into, but they are half open, and you can see everything.[18] In the

---

17 From an undated letter, probably written before December 7.
18 Umeko appears to be writing about public toilets.

family, too, you see many things such as dressing the children right before you and all. Shige said it was nice we came back in Winter because the nakedness of the coolies would not shock us so much as in Summer—even now I think nothing of bare legs way above the knees. The women often expose their breast in a horrid way—but I suppose all this is what Japanese would laugh about and think it as modesty, but still I can't bear to hear everything almost, talked about before men.[19]

Thursday
December 7, 1882

I am very glad, Mrs. Lanman, that you say you do not show my letters to but a very, very few. You know I write for you and Mr. Lanman alone, and there are few or none of my letters but what there is something for your ears *alone*. Do not show any of my letters to Japanese, please, for they might ridicule my criticisms of Japanese things. Even here in my half foreign home, they think many American ways and notions strange. . . . Oh women have the hardest part of life to bear in more ways than one. . . . Poor, poor women, how I long to do something to better your position! Yet why should I, when they are so well-satisfied, and do not seem to know any better? But I am told Japanese treat their wives with so much more deference than they did ten years I ago. I am so afraid all my desire and enthusiasm will be gone before I begin my work, for I must first learn the language and when that is done, I feel sure, I shall be too discouraged because I am getting so now.

---

19 From the letter of December 7, although this portion is omitted from *The Attic Letters*.

The situation has no doubt changed a good deal, both in Japan and in the West, in the century since Umeko came home. For example, public toilets were segregated at some point. Customs regarding the amount of skin that may be politely shown to the opposite sex, Western-style dresses that show off a woman's shoulders and arms, men and women dancing in each other's arms, women nursing their babies in public with breasts bared, half-naked laborers—both foreign and Japanese eyes have been astonished by many things, but it no longer makes sense to empathize with their shocked sensibilities.

Some decades ago, the attitudes and behavior of hippies all over the world may have been a revolt from within against the rigid mentality of the West. Bare feet and naked bodies in loincloths like Indian beggars, long hair and free sex—all were part of a rebellion against the hypocrisy that had taken root in the name of Western ideals, and this rebellion may well have been triggered by contact with the East, where such things are regarded as part of the eternal cycle of birth and death.

> One thing in Japan that is a little hard is what we might call freedom of speech. You know in America we don't discuss everything even in family but it is very different here. Many things are uncomfortable to hear talked about. The immoralities of people and everything. To discuss in open society the prospect of a baby is nothing at all. To request to go to W.C. is as common and natural as it is to ask for a drink of water.[20]

Umeko treated the frankness of the Japanese with a touch of humor, referring to it as "what we might call freedom of speech." This attitude would

---

20 From the same letter of December 7. Umeko asks Mrs. Lanman to keep this portion from Mr. Lanman's eyes, but it is doubtful that she succeeded.

seem to reflect not only the manners of the Lanman household, which nurtured her for eleven years, but also the tone of their whole social world. There is, however, room for thought as to whether the sensibilities of the Lanmans and their milieu were representative of American society in general. And of course, the Lanmans would have been especially careful in educating a foreign child entrusted to them by the Japanese government.

Charles Lanman was a government official who held various positions in the U.S. State Department, the Department of the Interior, and the Library of Congress. He published more than thirty books, including *The Private Life of Daniel Webster* (1852) and *The Japanese in America* (1872). His circle included men like Henry Longfellow, William Bryant, and Washington Irving. He was a secretary for the Japanese legation at one point, which led to his being entrusted with Umeko's care.

Adeline Lanman was the daughter of a successful businessman who presented her with a semi-detached house in Georgetown when she married. She and her husband lived in half of the duplex, where Umeko grew to adulthood.

Fishing and travel were among Charles Lanman's hobbies, and he appears to have been reasonably well off. The couple had no children of their own and loved Umeko like a daughter. During her long stay, she was taken on trips around the United States and lived in a house full of books. Clearly, she grew up with many advantages not available to the average American child.

CHAPTER
3
IMPATIENCE

December 14, 1882
[Azabu]

. . . It is too much of a difference, and I feel strange and do not yet feel accustomed or at home in this new life. Sometimes I say to myself is it possible that I am really in Japan and that this is the land and people that I have thought about so often. I suppose I will feel so some time yet, and then afterward America will seem like a dream, and a thing long past.

The other day, I much amused Father and Koto by telling them of American manners, especially as regards the treatment of ladies by gentlemen—how they gave up their seat in the cars, took off their hats when thanked, gave ladies privilege of bowing, acknowledging thus an introduction if she wished to keep up an acquaintance—how ladies got into carriages first, gentlemen after. It is so different in Japan, that they were much interested. Truly ladies here are not treated with one half that attention. It would be funny if in the Tokio streetcars, a gentleman got up to give his seat to a lady. And Shige warned us when we arrived that we must get used to [the] Japanese way, (what she called rudeness). I have not yet experienced any unpleasant ways, but I can not but feel the difference, and wish it were otherwise. But I must and do remember that in no place in the world do women have the liberty and respect as in America, and our women are so much better treated than those of any other Asiatic nation, that one should not expect too much. These little things we girls feel, and I tell you, but no one, not even missionaries, can understand exactly, for all foreigners live in a foreign circle with a home and comforts that are their own, but of course we are in regular Japanese homes, and see Japanese ways when just fresh from America. I tell you everything I think of, because I know you are interested, but you will not let other people, and especially Japanese from the Legation, see my opinions on many of these subjects, for they would only laugh at my many foreign notions. But you can appreciate it all. Even to my own family, who are indeed so kind and considerate, would I tell all I would tell you, because they can not understand how many things strike me. Tokio streets are many of them very dirty and my ears are saddened by the sound of coughing from these poor jinricksha men who pull me around. It is sad to see them and know that sooner or later they die. The life is so hard, especially in this cold weather, when they get so heated working, and then so suddenly cool off. And then they take cold, and it settles in their lungs, and so lays the foundation for consumption. But what we should do without jinrickshas in Tokio, I don't know.

Norms of courtesy between men and women have changed so greatly in different ways in Japan and the United States that young people today might be puzzled by Umeko's description of America. Older people, on the other hand, may feel a touch of nostalgia at hearing how things used to be in America, and then again in Japan. Feminists no longer appreciate having doors opened for them, or hats doffed, or seats given up to them. Such superficial acts have no merit; what they want is true freedom and equality.

Umeko's observations about missionaries are interesting. She was frequently critical of them, noting that they were arrogant and refused to mingle with the Japanese, looking down on them and barely speaking the language despite long years of living in Japan. Her sister Koto said there was not a single American who could speak polite Japanese, she reported.

The missionaries were preoccupied with sectarian differences. They were narrow-minded and could not appreciate anything that was not American. Anyone who could judge fairly should see that both countries had their merits, but these people had no eye for Japan's good points. They regarded all things American to be superior and disliked anything that was Japanese. Some had never tasted Japanese sweets and would never think of entering a Japanese restaurant. Umeko did not think Japanese cooking equal to American, but it was a fine cuisine nonetheless.

Japanese clothing had its drawbacks, but compared to the way American women forced their bodies into tight corsets, Japanese kimonos were not half so troublesome. They didn't look at all funny and had a general air of elegance and chic.

Some foreigners refused to take off their shoes in Japanese homes, which was a problem. Umeko's aunt and her sister Koto felt Umeko's waist and were appalled at how tightly she was corseted. There were many aspects of American manners that Japanese found intolerable, and Umeko grumbled that both sides should be more flexible and try to see the good in other people's ways.

Japanese saw that Westerners changed their underwear frequently and wondered if they were so unclean as to make this necessary. They witnessed their habit of using handkerchiefs and thought they should use disposable paper napkins rather than force someone to wash all those soiled hankies. Westerners thought Japanese kimonos showed too much leg too easily. Japanese found high-necked Western-style dresses much too constraining, although they regarded the cumbersome sashes that Japanese women wore around the waists of their kimonos—a custom that appalled Westerners— as a beautiful complement to the female figure. Little quirks and habits of daily life have remarkably deep roots that make them resistant to change. There are reasons behind them, linked to a long chain of other reasons, which is why it is so difficult to change a society or the way it educates its people. It is easy to imitate steam engines, ships, telegraph systems, navies, and armies, but changing the thoughts and sensibilities that underlie a way of life and its manners is another matter.

Umeko's letters are so vibrant that you can hear her voice as she makes you see the things she describes. She fastens her gaze on the sights before her and is awed and astonished at the way each scene pulsates with life. She is not so much impressed by the differences in manners as interested in the forces of life that she sees at work behind them. Superficial manners can change in a twinkling. In the West, long skirts that concealed women's legs became shorter; handkerchiefs were demoted to mere props and disposable tissues now litter the world. In Japan, fewer and fewer women wear kimonos with every passing year.

Of course, it is easy to imitate steam engines, ships, telegraph systems, navies, and armies, but what of the minds of the people who operate them? Japanese people learned to wear Western clothing and mastered the use of modern machinery, but their hearts are still stirred by Man'yō poetry composed more than a thousand years ago.

Be that as it may, Umeko's opinions about foreign people were little known until the discovery of her letters to Adeline. Now, having sensed young Umeko's resentment, I recall to myself that when she founded a school in her later years, she imbued it with elements of Christianity but did not make it into a mission school.

When I was a student at Tsuda College, religious services were conducted on campus as private gatherings and students were never required to attend. Bible study was compulsory for students majoring in English literature or language, but it was taught more as a work of literature than as a religious text.

Umeko also favored Japanese dress in her later years. She had a way of trying out the things she discovered in Japan and making them her own.

She repeated in letter after letter that new ideas could not be forced on the Japanese people and that it was reprehensible how missionaries had so little knowledge of Japanese ways and merely sat around criticizing them. Customs always had reasons behind them. Japanese were appalled when

Americans walked into a room wearing shoes that had walked over muddy streets, but they did not consider that American houses were designed so that most of the mud usually fell off or was scraped off as people approached the entrance, and that shoes touched only the floor of the rooms, where people had chairs to sit on. In the same way, Americans should observe Japanese customs more carefully before criticizing them, she wrote.

Over the past century Japanese and Americans customs have drawn closer to each other and been allowed to mix. It became fashionable some time ago for younger Americans to remove their shoes at home and sit on the floor, whereas in Japan, people wear their shoes at the office and sit in a chair at a desk. People still take off their shoes at home, but in 1989, it is entirely normal for Japanese homes to have beds, sofas, dining tables, desks, and chairs.

Umeko, on the other hand, was having trouble adapting to Japanese life and relearning Japanese. She worried about her future work and was distressed by things she saw and heard. She was sometimes angry, sometimes in despair, but she pulled herself up and dreamt of the future.

... There is a way of addressing inferiors, superiors, equals, and a very polite form—less so, and so on. So in one language one has to learn two or three. Then there are so many expressions with no meaning only polite form. So that I am puzzled. ...

Today I began the dreadful task of beginning to learn to write and read a few Chinese Characters. It makes me sick to think of how much I have to learn before I can read a newspaper even not to mention writing an ordinary letter of friendship. Then I have to learn to talk Japanese nicely and these foreigners do not after eight years residence and study. So you can imagine what a mountain it seems to me I have to climb.

I am having a dress made because I do not want to borrow Koto's and I must get used to the dress. They all make all manner of fun of me when I have it on, because my foreign underclothes make it get funny. And you see I can take off some things, drawers for instance, which go into stockings and my chemise too. Then they say my sleeves seem to be in my way and my dress does keep getting down, and open, and my obi untied, so I have such a time. But the other day I even put on Japanese clogs, fixing my stockings to suit the thong, I ran with the children in them.

Koto tried to put up my hair Japanese way, but could not—it was far too much. Yes, your little girl is transformed now, and you would laugh to see me in Japanese dress, but I am not half as Japanese as I am going to be—in fact not as much as Stematz,[1] for in her house there is nothing the least foreign and she complains that sitting Japanese way does tire her. Now with me, when I am home I need not sit that way at all, but I do. When I go visiting, my feet do get asleep, but in American dress I can fix myself comfortably and hide my clumsy feet, and then they are always considerate and keep asking me how I feel, but I prefer to sit on floor than alone in solitary glory in the only chair in the house, which is often offered me at various houses. I always refuse and do as much as I can Japanese way though it is very strange, far stranger than you can imagine—not only this but many other ways.

I was struck with the difference in the two countries, when I looked over my books to choose something for Koto to read. She could read far better in English than many Americans who read classics in other languages, but the curious allusions to manners, customs, way of living would keep her from appreciating and understanding many of the books I have. She could read essays, travels, or religious books, but not novels, descriptions of home life and American ways, especially American light talk and society. . . .

---

1   Sutematsu. Her friends also called her "Steam."

**Sunday
December 17, 1882**

. . . We have had serious talks on the subject of our work, and what is before us, with many people. They all ask what we want to do and many advise us a great deal. They expect so much from us, expect us to exert a great deal of influence, do much good, that it makes us feel very bad to think how little we can do. Many tell us that nothing is more needed than a school for girls where they could get sound education and accomplishments and be fitted to be wives of the great men. Our aim would be to reach higher classes, of course. Now we have many obstacles; among them prejudice against women's education, and then teaching is so cheap in Japan, and they refuse to pay more than a mere pittance and so we must have endowment or something to be able to keep up any institution. Of course, Sutematsu would take the lead and I might help. The school must be small at first, but we hope that we may see a fine school. These plans of course are visionary, and we have said nothing to anyone but our few friends. If we could do such a thing, it would be grand work, and we could do more in a little while, than years of teaching in normal or in any other government schools, where we would only spend a few hours each day.

December 23, 1882

I . . . thank my luck that I came home when I did, and so am yet young and able to learn more readily. If I had stayed in America much longer, it would have been harder and harder. Sutematsu, I think, must feel that she is considered old. Just think, I know a bride not fourteen, but such early marriages are after this year to be forbidden by law. Everyone asks how old we are, first thing, and in Japan it is not considered rude at all to ask, and we are old, for we are beyond the time when the average girl marries. Many of them are fifteen to sixteen, or seventeen to eighteen, Japanese way of counting, and as the Japanese old way of calculating is about two years [more] than the foreign and new way here, it is just the same as saying the average age of girls when married is from fourteen to sixteen. . . . I don't believe my Father is anxious or desirous of having me married, at any way for some time, as he never says anything about it, I do not worry myself at all, at my advanced age.[2] But an old maid is an unheard-of thing in Japan, and I guess there is no word in the language for spinster or old maid. Sutematsu and I inwardly lament over the fact that we shall do such an unprecedented thing as to live and die old maids. But we won't marry and don't care to, and if we did, we would find it hard, for Japanese husbands require so much attention and obedience and do not treat their wives with a bit of respect and love, if they have any. Of course, this is not always the case, but it is so in general.

December 24, 1882

. . . For you know that Japanese are much quieter and not so boisterous, quick, active, and noisy as Americans. So we must strike them as sort of rough and unrefined and not quiet, and unrestrained.

"We" refers to Sutematsu, Shige, and herself—the three returnees from abroad, who share a common obligation and vision with regard to their native country. She speaks here of the crude behavior of Americans, but she also wrote earlier that she must accustom herself to the crude manners

---

2   Almost eighteen.

of the Japanese. She was a good observer of the way crudity reveals itself in different ways in different places.

Umeko expresses herself in a way that seems full of contradictions at first. This can be confusing to the reader, but as I read her letters one after the other, I began to feel the charm of a style that follows the leaps and bounds of her very human heart. She shines the light of her mind on the same phenomenon from different angles, bouncing the light off of other things and other phenomena in order to observe its refractions, and in that way captures the complex webs and scope of human thought.

She frequently excuses herself after a comment, saying that she is writing her thoughts as they come to her, without correction, and that her letters are not to be shown to other people. But her words, contradictory as they may be, are interesting precisely because the contradictions form part of their appeal. Umeko had a supple sensibility that could pull her heart simultaneously in opposite directions.

> . . . I myself am struck with foreign noisy and flustering ways, though I have been here only one month and it seems to me out of place. I do not like the looks of foreigners. They seem so odd and after seeing Japanese costumes, the American dress looks incongruous just in the same way the Chinese look in Washington in their pink satins etc. In Rome do as the Romans, so for that reason if for no other I want to put on Japanese dress and look as if I were one of the people here. Now when I go shopping, quite a crowd gathers around me, but they never molest me or say one word, they only look with wide eyes and open mouths as long as I stand, when I go away they don't follow. This is a slight improvement on America but I do not like even this little bit.

Umeko was one of a tiny handful of young Japanese women students in Washington and was no doubt followed by many curious eyes. This was especially true when she arrived in San Francisco at the age of seven and traveled through Chicago to Washington, D.C. Americans stared at her as at a great novelty and crowded around her, sometimes touching her long-sleeved kimono and elaborate hair arrangement.

With memories like these, it must have been a profound experience to come home after eleven years in America, only to experience the same thing again. What was this, this going to and fro between two such different countries? What did it mean for the future of humanity? She must have pondered the answers to such questions by plumbing the depths of her own personal experience.

As recounted above, she already had visions of founding a private school, though it was only a month since her return to Japan. I wonder how much of her personal experiences during that time were woven into the fabric of those visions. In her dogged efforts to learn Japanese, she must have sensed the presence of the dark, endless depths of another world within that language. English contained another such world too, and she wanted the Japanese to discover it.

December 28, 1882

. . . We are very busy here making mochi (a kind of rice cake) for New Year's. At New Year's it is dreadful the number of presents that must be sent. To be sure they are not much—fruit, fish, candies but when so many have to be sent, it does amount to a great deal. For instance, there was sent to me on my arrival only thirty six presents or offerings in Congratulation, and every one of these have to be returned.

. . . The days are fast flying away and, in a few days, I shall be eighteen and the New Year begun. Well, I shall wish you, while I remember it, a very Happy New Year. . . . and though I often long to see you all again and be back in America, I would not have anything different, for I feel I must be of use. . . . Truly, there is much to be done for the women of Japan.

. . . I . . . take everything on the bright side, and it is well I do so. It is well, I have a happy disposition, because I see much unpleasant, and dark and gloomy are some of the clouds that shadow Japan. But there is a bright side too, and we will look upon it. To be sure they say now, the Conservative party is in power now, and there is much against progress and foreigners. But then, let us only consider this the reaction, consequent upon such a change as has taken place in the last twenty years.

Soon after this, Umeko wrote that they (Sutematsu and herself) had heard nothing from the Japanese government regarding their work and were worried that they had been forgotten.[3] Around the same time, a letter from Yamakawa Sutematsu to Alice Bacon[4] voiced a similar complaint.

As Umeko noted in the letter above, anti-Western sentiment was on the rise in Japan, foreigners were out of favor, and there was not much demand for the English language. The time had come to an end when all things foreign were considered with favor.

In 1882, the government reorganized the banknote system and adopted a deflationary policy in an attempt to combat the inflation that had plagued the nation since the Satsuma Rebellion.[5] Prices tumbled and farming

---

3   In a letter written after New Year, not included in *The Attic Letters*.

4   Sutematsu lived in New Haven in the home of the Rev. Leonard Bacon while she studied in the U.S. Alice was Bacon's daughter and became a lifelong friend of both Sutematsu and Umeko. Alice later came to Japan to help Umeko when she founded a school.

5   Taking place in 1877 and also called the War of the Southwest, this was the final stand of disaffected samurai against the new imperial government. It was called the Satsuma Rebellion because its charismatic leader, Saigō Takamori, was a native of Satsuma and the main battles took place in Satsuma (present-day Kagoshima) and neighboring Kumamoto.

communities were severely depressed, leading to an outbreak of peasant uprisings such as the Chichibu Incident[6] in November 1884, and the rise of the Freedom and People's Rights Movement.[7]

Umeko was distressed by the situation and despaired at her own powerlessness. Meanwhile, she complained that she was growing fat from eating so much Japanese food and rice, but she dressed up in a kimono and sent Mrs. Lanman a photograph.

Putting on a kimono was one thing, but both Umeko and Sutematsu were put off by the intricate Japanese hair arrangements that called for a great deal of hair wax and wooden pillows at night to keep the coiffeur in place, the shaving of all facial hair, the thick layer of white foundation on the face, and bright red rouge on the lips. Sitting on the floor in a kimono was also a problem, since the legs were not free to relax as within the shelter of a voluminous skirt.

Umeko disliked the feel of hair on her forehead and neck, and could not tolerate the face-shaving and heavy make-up considered necessary complements to wearing a kimono, so she decided to continue wearing Western-style clothing as part of her day-to-day attire.

In America, Mrs. Lanman had scolded her when she walked pigeon-toed and took very small steps, telling her it looked ugly. But here in Japan, walking in *geta* (Japanese clogs) with toes pointed outward was just as ugly as mincing pigeon-toed in America. If that was the case, Umeko thought, she would keep some of her American ways until her Japanese was up to par.

She faced difficulties like these, but they did not mean that she could not go on living in Japan, or that she wanted to return to America. But she

---

6   Although only one among dozens of riots in 1884, the Chichibu Incident was notable for its scope, its link to revolutionary ideology, and the fierceness with which it was put down.

7   This was a movement for social and political reform that reached its zenith in the mid 1880s. It succeeded in exerting pressure on the Meiji government toward a show of democratic reform, but failed to establish the true democracy it hoped to achieve.

did feel nostalgic for her days in America, when Japanese language and manners were not a problem and she could simply dream about returning to Japan and living there.

The Japanese language was difficult. There were so many ways to say the same thing that it made her head spin, and she felt that she was always being goaded into using "some long-winded, intangible, incomprehensible sentence."[8] This in itself is proof of her sensitivity to language, for it is the essence of Japanese in a nutshell. However, Umeko lamented her lack of a gift for languages. In fact, she kept her diary in English to the end of her days and appears to have remained more comfortable in that language, at least when she was writing.

As I have noted, Umeko had the precise observational skills of a scientific mind. She also had an admirable writing style that expressed complex emotions in a nuanced way, conveying them as living and moving things. Charles Lanman, who had a long writing career behind him, evidently thought she had talent, and repeatedly pressed her to publish her letters and diary. She could no doubt have done so with his help, but she felt that she was able to express her innermost thoughts precisely because she was writing to the couple privately, and she remarked to Lanman that she would rather refrain from making public anything other than what she specifically wrote for publication. In fact, she stated emphatically at one point that if he intended to show her letters to others, henceforth she would write only model letters filled with platitudes.

Umeko believed to the end of her life that she never quite mastered Japanese, and there are indications that others agreed. This was due to her extreme sensitivity to language and an aversion to merely imitating

---

8   In a letter dated January 6, 1883.

the words she heard, I think. The reason her English did not deteriorate in spite of her long years in Japan is because she was a great reader, and because she never forgot to look for what lies beneath the words.

In later years, she translated into English excerpts from Japanese classics such as the *Heike monogatari* (The Tale of the Heike), *Taiheiki* (Chronicle of Great Peace), *Genpei seisuiki* (Rise and Fall of the Minamoto and Taira Clans), a number of kyōgen plays, and Higuchi Ichiyō's *Jūsan'ya* (The Thirteenth Night), all of which were published in *Eibun shinshi* (The Student), a reader for students of English.

Umeko was always interested in new publications of English and Japanese literature and shuttled between her two languages almost to the point of obsessiveness. Her reading habits stemmed back to her childhood and adolescence, when she was the only child in the household of Charles Lanman—himself a writer—where it was the custom to read until bedtime. Adeline frequently sent her novels and Umeko diligently jotted down her impressions after reading them. Her parents, Sen and Hatsuko, were also capable writers, so Umeko was born into an environment that sensitized her to language.

Soon after Umeko arrived in the United States at the age of seven, Adeline Lanman wrote to her mother Hatsuko. Appended below are Adeline's letter, Hatsuko's reply, and a letter written (in Japanese) by little Umeko to her mother.[9]

---

9 The three letters are cited, in Japanese, in *Tsuda Umeko bunsho*, 85–89, and in Yoshikawa, *Tsuda Umeko den*, 60–66.

Mrs. Lanman's letter:[10]

Your daughter Ume, together with Yoshimasu Ryō, is now living in the second story of our home. Both are under our care and happy. My husband is a secretary attached to the Japanese Legation, which is in our neighborhood. Last Tuesday, the Japanese mission arrived in Washington, where the commissioner, Mr. Mori, and others awaited them. Everything went well, and my husband's sister promised that she would take care of the girls. Your daughter will live with us for a while. She is too young to go directly to a boarding school, so until Mr. Mori directs us otherwise, she will be entrusted to our care. Teiko, Sutematsu and Shigeko will live nearby. My sister-in-law and husband will visit both places daily and assist them. All of the girls are admirably eager to learn. Ume is especially quick and all who meet her admire and praise her manners. They are saying that she has no doubt been very well brought up. We are all delighted with Ume, and say that her mother willingly permitted her dear daughter to be taken so far away because heaven has given her great gifts. We are grateful to you for entrusting such a daughter to the care of foreigners, and we look upon her as a gift from heaven. We are already very fond of Ume and if in the future we are obliged to part from her, we are already worried about how sad we shall be. The day your diplomatic mission arrived was a joyful one for our country. This will surely create a stronger tie between our two nations. I know that your

---

10 The letter was written in English, but the original has been lost. Tsuda Sen is thought to have translated it into Japanese for his wife. The letter presented here is a reverse translation from the Japanese.

people are already well disposed toward our people. On our side as well, the more Japanese friends we make, the fonder we grow of the Japanese and the more we like Japan. The night that Ume arrived in this city, she came straight to our home and was made comfortable. In order that you may know what kind of people will be caring for her, I enclose a photograph of ourselves so that you may see us. The photos she was given before her departure she likes very much and often takes them out to look at. Particularly the one of her sitting beside you, she often shows to the people around her. Ume sends you her deepest regards. Please give my best wishes to your husband.

Respectfully yours,
Mrs. Charles Lanman
March 4, 1872

Hatsuko's reply:[11]

I read with great pleasure your detailed letter of March 4, 1872. Before all else, please allow me to express my happiness that both you and your husband are well and prospering. We are very grateful and very happy and relieved to know in detail how, through the mysterious workings of fate, Ume, together with Yoshimasu O-ryō-sama, is in the second story of your home and being cared for with such kindness. I learned that Mr. Mori was there expressly to greet the diplomatic mission as it arrived in your country, that all proceeded so excellently, and I think that those who undertook this journey for the first time must have found all to be new and strange. We read in the newspapers of your welcome and were very grateful. That your

---

11 The English translation sent to Adeline has been lost.

husband and his sister should undertake to care so well for the girls and that they are eagerly pursuing the study of English, I am humbly gratified to learn. O-tei-sama, Sutematsu-sama and O-shige-sama will be nearby, but I understand that Ume, being too young to go to school will be under your care for a while. I am grateful that you have condescended to take her under your care in your home, as she will undoubtedly cause you concern. I leave everything to your discretion and beg you to educate her as strictly as you judge necessary. She has so many siblings that I believe she will grow up in better circumstances than if she had remained by my side. I learned from O-ryō-sama that you play with her as if she were a child of your own flesh and blood, and for this my indebtedness is deeper than the sea. My brush cannot possibly express the extent of my gratitude. I thank you very much for your photograph and that of your home. It is as if I am seeing you in person and we have gathered to look at it together.

I am happy to learn that your people welcome visitors from my land with such hospitality. Here, clothing, food, and all things from your country grow in reputation day by day. It is already a while since we have had a telegraph and a railroad and things have become so much more convenient that your people are looked upon more favorably than ever before. In the years ahead I should like to meet you and express my gratitude to you in person. That Ume is taking out the photos I gave her when she departed and is looking at them, but not expressing any desire to return to her country, I am certain is due to the great delicacy of your treatment.

We are relieved to know that O-ryō-sama is well, that you are treating Ume with such kindness, and that you will always be there to help and to advise her. Once again at the end of this letter, I thank you on behalf of both Ume and myself. I will write again. Today, I write but briefly in reply.

I pray that you will keep yourself well in the coming season. In the photographs you sent us, we noticed that you have many framed pictures. I wish to present you with some photos of famous places in Japan and hope that you will accept them with a smile. Again I send you warm wishes on behalf of us all and thank you again and again.

> Respectfully yours,
> from Mr. and Mrs. Tsuda
> to the honorable wife of Mr. Charles Lanman
> April 17

Letter from Umeko to her mother:

I send you greetings. Before all else, I am happy to find you all together and well. I am also well and happy and beg you to rest easy regarding this point. As I have already written, I arrived with all my companions in Washington. We had been learning from a lady named Miss Lauren, and when she returned to her home, another teacher came to us and has been giving us lessons from ten o'clock to twelve o'clock. This place is about thirteen chō[12] from the home of Mr. Lanman and Miss Lanman also comes here frequently, so please do not worry. O-ryō-san intended to send a reply, but her eyes are ailing and she is also resting from her lessons, and as she cannot answer your letter, I am writing in her stead.

I am reading my first book.

---

12 1 *chō* = 109 meters.

I am just beginning to read about the Earth. I am also beginning to practice writing. Please rest easy about me.

> Ume
> to my mother
> Please take care of yourself.
> Respectfully yours.

I am taken back to my days at Tsuda College, when Japanese writing, creative English writing, and translation from Japanese to English were required courses, with small classes of about twenty students each. We had to hand in papers every week, which were invariably checked in great detail, marked and given back to us. This must have been a tradition established by Umeko, and it was distinctive to our school. I wonder if the tradition is still carried on.

CHAPTER
4
FRETTING

For eighteen-year-old Umeko, the problem of marriage was a pressing one. For one thing, Japanese girls were married off at an abnormally young age. Then, young men and women had discouragingly few opportunities to socialize, and furthermore, once married, a woman had no purpose in life but to care for her children and work devotedly for her husband and his family. That was her whole life, and Umeko wondered if it was enough.

Few of the Japanese men Umeko had known in America came to call on her, and women in Japan could not go out alone. Umeko could accompany other women if they went out, but in those days, proper young ladies were expected to take a jinricksha. Umeko had a good appetite and tended to put on weight, and even a stretch of fine weather made her fret about the link between the climate and the indolence of the Japanese people.

She was baffled by the Japanese language, which had no evident grammar, system, or rules which required her to memorize everything. Western clothing was difficult to buy, but the few articles she possessed were growing tighter and tighter as she put on weight. The Japanese government had lost interest in the student returnees and gave them no work to do.

Why in the world had they been sent to study in America for ten years at the expense of the Japanese people? Obsessing about the idea of improving society was like standing before a mountain that could not possibly be climbed. And on top of all this, she was eighteen years old in a social environment where marriage was a bleak option.

January 6, 1883

... Do you know how many marriages are made between people who do not even know the slightest of each other's characters? A man has a vague idea of marrying and tells someone to look out for a suitable wife. And this "go-between" fixes it with the family and parents and then they have a meeting and look at each other. If satisfactory to all, the engagement is made, and marriage follows soon after. An engagement is usually as sacred as marriage, and to break one off would be very bad, and lead others to suppose that some secret reason existed against either the man or woman—usually the woman gets the blame. I presume then the only true love matches are when these men—mostly great men—marry the singing and dancing girls of the lowest class, for they are truly beautiful and many are accomplished, for they live merely to please. How can love matches be made, when gentlemen never call on ladies, and there is so little society where the men and women mingle? To be sure, men do come to see the family, father or brother, and the women may be about, but they generally keep back. When company stay to dinner, as they do often here, the family never eat with them. If Father's guests, he eats; if mine, Father and I eat, but the others wait on us. . . . Talk of reform in society, men and women must be more educated, cultivated, and be better, to mingle, especially with the women. . . .

January 16, 1883

. . . Sutematsu, Shige, and I have had some serious talks on the subject of marrying. An unmarried woman can truly do very little. Women do not have much freedom anyway, but an unmarried one still less. They seem to think both of them (which is *very* hard), that we must decide now whether we are willing to live single all our lives or not, because if we do marry, and want to be married, we will have chances now, that we will not have a few years from now, because then all the men will be married. It is too dreadful, but as I feel now I would not marry unless I wanted to, no matter if I have to live like a hermit, and nothing would induce me to make a regular Japanese marriage, where anything but love is regarded. I am sure that Father would not make me, and as I don't know Japanese ways at all, and, above all, have not had anything said to me on the subject, nor any offers, I am not going to worry in spite of Shige's lectures and Sutematsu's warnings as to my age. But I am glad nevertheless that I am as young as I am, and wish I was still younger. Most people in Japan would laugh at the idea of love marriages and think them dreadful. Japanese women are so dutiful to their husbands and do so much for them that unless we were *truly* loved, we could never get along, because, as Shige says, we never can be so deferential, obedient, and respectful, and polite as they. Then mothers-in-law are all powerful in Japan. . . . I will not marry just to get married as most Japanese do, and as Father is very kind he will not make me. In Japan it is considered all right for parents to make marriages, but never does a young man write or address a woman, or even speak to the father. He must always get someone to speak to the family for him, tell about his affairs, his business, etc., and then the father, if he chooses, and when he is thoughtful, consults the daughter. Even Mr. Uriu engaged to Shige in America had to have someone formally ask Mr. Masuda, and he asked Shige. . . . There is no such word as courting, flirting, in Japanese. . . . So I will dismiss the subject until I am twenty, which gives me two years, anyway, of liberty. . . .

"Courting"—where a man woos a woman—and "flirting"—by which a woman indicates her interest—do not exist as words in Japanese, she laments. Later, by teaching English and other foreign languages, she would try to show Japanese women that there are different ways of thinking about the world.

Americans and Japanese are all unquestionably human, living creatures, and obviously have gestures and behaviors designed to attract the opposite sex. There are phrases in Japanese such as "send a glance like an autumn wave," "cast an amorous glance," "beguile," "be willing," or "make a pass," but they are not used all that commonly. On the other hand, saying something like "he is being kind to her" is vague, but loaded with meaning. Ambiguity may be the soul of the Japanese language, so its way of expressing sexual interest can be regarded as part of its cultural flavor.

Shortly before writing the letter above, Sutematsu and Umeko had been invited, as friends of Shigeko and her husband, to attend a party at the home of Kanda Naibu, who had been studying abroad at the same time as the girls and who was still single. Kanda was apparently interested in Sutematsu, and a letter from Sutematsu to Alice Bacon suggests that he made a marriage proposal of sorts.

Soon afterwards, Kanda played a scene from Shakespeare's *Merchant of Venice* together with Sutematsu, Shigeko, Umeko, and Shigeko's husband Uriu, as part of the entertainment at Shigeko's wedding banquet—a party held sometime after the wedding itself. The banquet was hosted by Shigeko's elder brother Masuda Takashi, president of Mitsui & Co., and attended by various high government officials. The girls disliked the usual entertainment at such affairs, provided by geishas and other professionals, so they put together the play as an alternative.

So the "serious talks" between the three—Shigeko, apparently happy in a love-marriage of sorts with a man she met in America, Sutematsu, who was considering marriage in a fairly specific context, and Umeko, with no specific marriage plans at all—amounted to a strategic conference to deal with the contemporary marriage situation.

Sutematsu played Portia in the *Merchant of Venice*. She was seen by Ōyama Iwao, the minister of the army, who took a liking to her and asked for her hand in marriage. Sutematsu apparently refused Kanda before her decision to marry Ōyama, but later recommended Kanda as a marriage partner for Umeko and asked Shigeko's elder brother to act on his behalf.

Kanda was willing and probably proposed to Umeko at some point.

Around this time, Sutematsu frequently mentioned Umeko in her letters to Alice Bacon, noting that Umeko's father was an eccentric who kept Umeko at home in lonely isolation and that the only way to save her was to marry her off. Sutematsu and Shigeko's perception of Umeko reached Adeline, who worried and wrote several letters recommending a number of men other than Kanda. Umeko refused adamantly each time and finally became angry, furiously insisting that she never wanted to hear the word marriage again, and more or less turned her back on the matter.

May 26, 1883

. . . She [Shige] gives you a wrong impression entirely. Firstly, she says I am lonely. In a sense, that is true. Do you remember that we three girls are entirely different from any Japanese in education, ideas, and experiences, that our ways of thinking and doing are so different, and consequently we are alone among the women of Japan? At the same time, she can not rightly say I am lonely when I do have pleasant friends, and a dear sister and happy family. And I did not ever hide from you that very often I think of America as a dear place and of you all. I think it very unwise and wild of Shige to write you such a letter. . . And if Shige said I did not go out much, she could not mean to parties, because I am not asked much, but perhaps she meant to go and see people. And I can't go to see people so very much, as it takes time to visit, and I am not very fond of formal calls, besides being busy at home. And Shige thinks my father is strict, does she? For a *Japanese* father he is one of the most indulgent, and *especially* so to me, because he knows I am brought up different, but Shige must have gotten the idea that he was so because I always ask him before I do anything, even stay at her house, and ask him when I go out, but as

Shige did not live with her father, nor Sutematsu either, she thinks it an unusual restraint. Oh, if you knew some Japanese daughters!!

. . . I am sorry to disappoint such indefatigable matchmakers as Shige, Sutematsu and you, but I guess I won't marry to please anyone. Please don't write anything about Mr. Serata. I always laughed at such an idea, and at him, for I don't even like him particularly, and poor and everything—one might imagine I was in love with him from you and Mr. Ueno. If you had arranged it or someone, you might have gotten me in a mess, if anyone really thought I cared. . . . I have no desire to marry at all, so we will say no more, if you please, on the subject. . . Don't let me discuss this any more.

. . . If I could only do my own way, and not have everybody think me strange, just because I am not married. But that is one of the trials—and trials have to come.[1]

Umeko's remonstrations to Adeline are more like what a girl might say to an intimate older friend than what she would say to her mother. She is straightforward and maintains a healthy balance between affection and cold reasoning. She is determined not to hear any more talk of marriage, and she also asserts that however difficult things are in Japan, she will not be a "coward and deserter"[2] and fly back to America, even if it were the easier thing to do. There would be no satisfaction or pleasure for her in leaving Japan. She would surely visit America again, but it would be only a visit. Now that she had seen the world from a wider perspective by being in Japan, she might be irritated or disappointed by the frivolities and scandals of American women, she adds.

---

1 In *The Attic Letters,* this last paragraph is placed at the end of a letter dated June 6, 1883.

2 These words and the following assertions are stated in the letter dated May 27, 1883.

Umeko's tone is fierce, passionate, and equally merciless in her criticism of both Japan and America. I take my hat off to the Lanmans, who fostered a foreign-born girl for ten years and nurtured a mind that could write a letter like this. As for Sutematsu's marriage, Umeko wrote as follows:

March 27, 1883

. . . The secret is no longer a profound secret and Sutematsu says I may tell. This is it. . . . In a few months, perhaps prolonged to six, Sutematsu has promised to marry *Mr. Oyama*, the Minister of the War Department, and one of the Imperial cabinet, besides a great General. . . . Need I say that this is a regular Japanese marriage? But Sutematsu was allowed freedom in her choice, and she decided for herself, though she grew thin with worrying and pondering and wavering, because it took much thought and foresight and resolution to do as she has, because it is for a lifetime. It was simply whether she would choose this or be poor and be more independent and free alone. Sutematsu knows the position and she has thus decided. Although this all took place a month ago, the regular engagement ceremony only takes place this week, and Sutematsu can now no more change the decision than if she were really married. Many persons know it, and a broken engagement causes scandal, and Sutematsu's fate is truly decided. Mr. Masuda, Shige's brother, was the go-between and this was all fixed so long ago, and I have been wild to tell you, but did not want to until Steam[3] gave me permission. Of course, in this match no love is thought of. They had only seen each other a short while when Sutematsu decided, but not without much thought, I can tell you, and how Shige and she and I discussed it. I will tell you all

---

3   The girls' nickname for Sutematsu.

about it. Of course, I can't help being sorry that the marriage is not for love, but she could hardly have made a love match in Japan. Men don't see enough of the women to fall in love, and it is a rare case to marry for love anyhow, and she respects and likes him, and so that is right. Then Sutematsu will not teach, of course; for the government, a *sangi's*[4] wife teaching would be absurd, and I am sorry to lose her help when I teach, for I must teach all alone. Then again Sutematsu will go out of our sphere and rank, be above us, and though she will never look down on us, yet I can't see as much of her as I do of Shige now after marriage. And she will be rather isolated as a great lady. But she can do wonderful good as a *sangi's* wife, when all the other great men's wives are former *geishas*, and she can help Japan. . . . It seems like a providential circumstance that he should just happen to be unmarried at Sutematsu's return, and that this chance is offered her. And he is, we are sure of it, what hardly one of the prominent men are, perfectly moral in every way, though not a Christian. He never drinks, or does any of those dreadful things others do, and he is very pleasant, and I am sure very, very kind. And so under the circumstances, Sutematsu, though in one of the hardest positions that a young girl was ever placed in, has done what she thought was best, seconded by her friends, Mr. Uriu, Shige and I among them.

. . . She will always have a carriage, a luxury for Japan, and there is a magnificent grand Parisian piano in the house and lots and lots of servants, and policemen always at the gate. . . Her dresses will be ordered from Paris, I guess, and she will have many nice things after she is married. . . .

---

4   A government minister.

April 11, 1883

. . . Well, I must tell you that Mr. Oyama according to foreign custom sent Sutematsu a ring—and a diamond ring at that. It has three shining brilliants, set beautifully, and is from Switzerland. These are not the last gems she will get, either. The time we went to Mr. Oyama's we had a lovely foreign dinner cooked very Frenchy and of about ten or more courses. There were about fourteen guests—Mr. Masuda, Shige's brother, Mr. and Mrs. Yoshida, Mrs. Saigo, Mr. Yano and some others. After dinner we played cards. The house is lovely, the rooms are large and furnished in the French way—in fact the house was made by a French architect just like the German Legation. Of course, we only saw a few rooms on the lower floor, but there are three stories in all, and quite spacious. At the entrance of the ground there are lamps, and soldiers at the gate and policemen around. General Saigo's home is next door, the Foreign Department near. The Russian and the German Legations right by, the English not far off. In fact, the elite of the city live in Nagata-cho. Although the engagement is not yet announced, many people are going to see Sutematsu and inviting her out, on account of the position she will have. Many of the *sangis'* wives are calling on her, and she is busy seeing and returning calls, and in going out. . . .

April 13, 1883

. . . Sutematsu will be in a position to do much good and influence many, and I hope and trust she will make use of her influence and rank for the good of Japan. . . .

So she reports on Sutematsu's impending marriage and meanwhile grows more skeptical about her own. Each time she witnesses another marriage at close range, she seems to take a step closer to life as a single woman.

Around the same time, Sutematsu was writing to Alice Bacon, youngest daughter of the family with whom she lodged while in America. She and Alice were close in age and Sutematsu wrote to her about her decision to marry Ōyama Iwao. Unmarried women in Japan were so powerless, Sutematsu reasoned, so if a woman hoped to do something for society, the most expedient way was to benefit from the influence of a powerful husband. It was not a love match, but she liked Ōyama. She would change that liking to love and respect and realize her own intentions and dreams through her husband.

If, in the future, Umeko desired to do something for the education of Japanese women, she was determined to support that enterprise in the role of Madam Ōyama, who would have much more power than an unmarried female educator named Yamakawa Sutematsu.

Just as Umeko kept up a correspondence with Adeline Lanman to the end of Adeline's life, Sutematsu continued to nurture her friendship with Alice, daughter of the Bacons of New Haven, even after she returned to Japan. Years later, this friendship led Alice to give enormous support to Umeko's school in the early years after its founding.

In 1980, a century after Sutematsu returned from her studies abroad, her great-granddaughter Kuno Akiko acquired several dozen letters written by Sutematsu to Alice, and in 1988, she published a book entitled *Rokumeikan no kifujin Ōyama Sutematsu* (Ōyama Sutematsu, Lady of Rokumeikan).[5]

Shortly after Kuno acquired Sutematsu's letters, NHK (Japan Broadcasting Corporation) took up her story in a documentary series called *Rekishi e no shōtai* (Invitation to History). Because of my interest in Tsuda Umeko, I was given the opportunity to read the original letters.

---

5   Kuno Akiko. *Rokumeikan no kifujin Ōyama Sutematsu* [Ōyama Sutematsu, Lady of Rokumeikan] (Tokyo: Chūō Kōronsha, 1988).

Reading and comparing Sutematsu and Umeko's letters, I was impressed at how the two women, living in the same era, each earnestly devoted their intertwined lives to building a future for Japan by different means.

Sutematsu was born in Aizu[6] to the Yamakawa family, her father a senior retainer of the Aizu domain. When the Meiji government recruited young girls to study abroad, the Yamakawa family dispatched Sutematsu, then twelve years old, to pursue the vision of the new woman. Her childhood name was "Sakiko," but her mother, distraught at sending her young daughter to a strange, faraway land, changed her name to "Sutematsu" before letting her go. *Suteru* (throw away) and *matsu* (wait) expressed the tender hope that what she "threw away" would come back to her if she waited long enough.

When Sutematsu returned to Japan eleven years later with Tsuda Umeko, Minister of the Army Ōyama Iwao had recently become a widower with three young daughters. He submitted a proposal of marriage to Sutematsu, but the Yamakawa family and the people of Aizu were understandably opposed to the match. This was because Ōyama, originally a retainer of the Satsuma domain, had fought on the side of the imperial government in the civil war that overthrew the Aizu clan and destroyed Aizu Castle.

Sutematsu was aware of these circumstances, but chose to accept the proposal of her own will. She was eight years old when government forces laid siege to the castle—old enough to recall the episode for an interview published in 1904 in the American journal *The Twentieth Century Home*.

The following are excerpts from letters written to Alice Bacon regarding her marriage to Ōyama:[7]

---

6   A city in present-day Fukushima that was the center of the former Aizu domain.

7   The author referred to Kuno's book for the letters and cited the Japanese translations, but the excerpts here are taken directly from transcripts of the original letters, kindly made accessible to us by Ms. Kuno.

. . . Oh, Alice my views on various subjects change so rapidly. I see now the necessity for Japanese women to be married. It is very different from America—this question of marriage. You can not tell till you have been in Japan and be a Japanese, but really it is necessary. I don't know but I shall have to come to the matrimonial state myself. (February 20, 1883)

. . . People talk of dying for one's country as a glorious thing, but to me, to live for one's country seems infinitely more self-sacrificing. If it is possible that by the death of someone Japan could be benefitted in some way I would willingly, rather gladly be that one, but that is impossible. What Japan needs is the life-long services of those who have her interest more at heart. . . .

I have no prospects of teaching in school and I am thoroughly disgusted with the whole concern. The Japanese are so slow and the government does not seem to care whether we teach or not. It is its own loss but it does not seem to care. There is nothing that I can do but to teach privately in a small way and do the best I can. (March 19, 1883)

. . . By the way do you remember I told you that I had an offer from a gentleman in a rather high position. Well, he has asked me again and I am thinking of it. There does not seem to be any position that I can fill and the mere teaching is not what Japan needs most. What must be done is a change in the existing state of society and this can only be accomplished by married women. I mean that I do not think that teaching is the only way to benefit Japan. If I thought that, if I did not teach, I would be perfectly useless to Japan. I would not hesitate to devote my whole life to teaching, but I feel sure that I can do some service to the country by giving up my pet plan.

Of course, I would not marry, either, just because I can do some good, but I am considering this subject not only for Japan's account but also on my own. It would not be right to make myself perfectly miserable just because I think I can do some good but it is possible that I may be happier and at the same time become more useful.

Alice, sometimes I get so troubled and I cannot tell what is right or what is wrong. (April 5, 1883)

. . . Mr. Ōyama was very urgent about making our engagement public, and so after considering the matter very carefully for two weeks, I have consented and we are formally engaged. Of course according to the Japanese custom, the usual ceremony of engagement took place and now we are bound to keep to our promises as if we were married. I would never take such a step without due consideration and I think I have done right.

He is so thoroughly good that I am sure I may trust my future to him. I suppose you will not like it and I have thought over that too, but I felt that in questions of this nature one can not hope to please everybody. I felt somehow that I was ungrateful to you but I know that you are too generous to think so. Besides you would not wish that this feeling should prevent me from doing what I think would be more for my future happiness and welfare.

Now I have something to look forward to and the feeling that one is necessary to someone's comfort and happiness is a wonderful cure for the worst blues and cheers me up to any kind of exertion. Although they all love me at home, I am not absolutely needed at home and the feeling that if I were dead, people would miss me but not mourn for me for very long used to make me very blue indeed, but now it is different. I have someone whose happiness is in my keeping and whose children's welfare is in my hands.

I do not mind all the small trials now come to me, for I don't pay them any attention but you have minded what it is to be wholly mis-understood sometimes. . . .

I hope to devote myself to my future husband's interests and try in every sense to be his helpmate. I feel that it is a very serious thing and I hope with God's help I shall be able to do my duty. . . . (July 2, 1883)

Whatever Umeko thought of Sutematsu's decidedly unconventional approach to marriage, she grew more and more doubtful about marriage in general as she saw at close quarters the way it was conducted in Japanese society. She wondered about the children born of such marriages and watched carefully to see what kind of men and women they would grow up to be. Half a year had gone by since her return to Japan.

May 13, 1883

. . . We have had, too, lately, many, many visitors recently, and they all take dinner here as a matter of course, never refusing a meal, and coming and staying at meal time. I sometimes say what would Mrs. Lanman, who bothers so about having everything *just so*, for one guest, *expected*—think of having ten come in, without warning, and dinner to give to all. They are always men, Father's friends, and I never meet them, or any of us women either, but we have to wait on them. Men are the only visitors. Men's parties are the only ones in Japan. Women are as quiet and lazy as cats, about doing anything for themselves. They are only waiters for men. I must say I wish the women took a little more important part in the doings of a house in Japan, beyond the feeding and providing part. Japanese women can not talk or entertain anyone of the opposite sex. . . . And if you could only see and understand what puzzles, bothers and perplexes me, but it is not possible for you or anyone to.

My heart does go out to Japanese women, and I burn with indignation at their position, while I blame them too. Japanese men I can not blame, because they are spoiled, brought up and treated to lord over the sisters and mothers, and afterwards their wives. And the women expect no better either. Oh, Mrs. Lanman, you can not know how I feel!! No one can understand, either in America or here, Japanese women are contented enough. . . . It is so rooted and ground into them. Their ways of thinking and acting, their foolish fear of appearing manlike, their ignorance and superstition and their slowness, and they don't expect better treatment from men—they feel they are inferior, and don't try to rise at all. It is not all in education that is wrong; the whole atmosphere must be changed. Children do see and understand many things they ought not to—one family trying to be different is like swimming against the tide, which will be sure to drown one. The very root is wrong, and so, though I feel it and bewail it, I can do nothing, I only fold my hands and shut my eyes. . . . I can not do anything, and I feel I am just going with the rest. . . . Do you know, children hear so much they ought not, and there is nothing good to teach them. The Japanese stories are immoral, and for a child like Fuki, of ten years, not fit to be touched. If you don't let her read them, there is nothing to supply the place—no Sunday school stories, no fairy tales or romances of a good kind. English is the only medium to get to this literature, and English takes years to learn. . . . If I thought that by my dying I could elevate these daughters of Japan, I should be glad to do so, but this you must not consider noble or heroic, or a sign that I am working and trying. Is it not easier to give up life, and see a work *done* than to blindly grope and try, and see the end unattained, and fret and worry over impossibilities? I am doing nothing in spite of my desire, I can not do anything, it seems, so I only want to get along, and be an *old selfish creature*.

. . . Now that we have sent away Yona's nurse she will sleep here after with me, and I am trying to get her accustomed. She will be in my room, in the bed. Yona is very cunning and I am very fond of her, but she is a very funny child indeed. In some ways she seems beyond her years. She is very smart, but very obstinate and self willed (like all of us) and hence a little hard to manage, but I think I will get along. I am a little disappointed in Japanese ways of bringing up children. It is true that my childish recollections were true for mother was strict then with me, like so many people with first children, but now she hates to thwart or punish any of the children and when they cry, they always give them candy to make them stop, so that candy or cake is munched all day. The filial obedience demanded for trivial things in life, begins when the child grows to girlhood, but neither my Father nor Mother are strict—in fact they are very easy, and with me it is very different from Japanese daughters. I could not be so good, but they don't expect it—not that I ever disobey, but I exercise my own judgement, as I should, to some degree. But Japanese little children have a good time, it is the best part of their life, and certainly they play in the open air, and enjoy their loose clothes, and eat candy, and get dirty, to their heart's content. It is so easy to get along in a house where one may roll on the floors, and have nothing to knock against. Japan is a paradise for children, as far as their enjoyment is concerned, as for their physical and mental health—that is another thing.

Umeko was the second daughter in a brood of twelve siblings and had many young brothers and sisters when she returned to Japan. It did not trouble her to play with them and she seems to have enjoyed it. Her mother Hatsuko was often ailing in the period after Umeko's return and was in and out of bed. Umeko mentions in passing that Hatsuko was up and about only two or three days out of the month when she was doing poorly and she seems to have gone away for spa cures at times like these. A younger sister named Kiyoko was born in December of 1881, the year before Umeko's return, and after her return, another sister, Tomiko, was born in 1884. It is possible that the mother was suffering from morning sickness and other problems relating to pregnancy and childbirth.

One elder sister and most of her younger siblings, as well as an aunt who lived with them, and numerous other relatives feature in many of Umeko's letters to Adeline. There is no indication that she found the large family irksome, and though she never married, she looked after family members and was looked after by them, maintaining a close relationship with siblings, nephews, and nieces throughout her life. They were very supportive of her in later years, with regard to the management of her school and in her private life. One reason she was never the lonely unmarried educator was no doubt because she was surrounded by their warm presence. Watching her young siblings grow up may also have helped to develop her principles as an educator.

August 12, 1883

...They [Umeko's younger brothers] are glad enough to be home from school. Jiro next winter will go to Kioto to school in Motochika's place, as he graduated this June. You could not believe Motochika is younger than I, it seems impossible when he is so tall—as tall as father. I often wish he could go to America and take a college course. He would like it, and he would like America. And I preach to him (you may laugh) about being polite to ladies and to the weaker one. I say women can do the serving and the easy muscular work, but when it comes to hard pulling and lifting, the men must help, so I make him shut the heavy wood doors of the upstair rooms and my room at night, and put away his own bed. If there is a heavy bench to be lifted, I ask Jiro to please do it and to help, and Koto and I agree it is only what they ought to do, and learn to do to help their elder sisters. And they are very good, and don't demur, though custom is on their side not to do it. They are willing boys, and very good, but seem old for their age. They think, however, when I tell them, that what they do in America is funny and peculiar. But then, they are much advanced for Japanese, and I think they study well too. I am very ambitious indeed for them.

Hoping that her little brothers would not grow up into pampered men who looked down on women, like the ones she saw around her, Umeko was dreaming of a future society where men and women cooperated and enjoyed life together.

In any case, she was disgusted with her own lack of progress in Japanese even months after her return to Japan, which may have had to do with the presence of her father and sister Koto, who spoke English to her. Sutematsu and Shigeko were older than Umeko and remembered more Japanese from their childhood, and therefore regained their language more quickly. Umeko compared herself to them and bemoaned her own slowness and stupidity.

Umeko also reported that she had been offered a teaching job at the Methodist church through an introduction from Shigeko, and that she would take the position for a month and a half during the summer.

May 25, 1883

. . . I don't want to teach for missionaries, and should not do it as regular work, for somehow I feel that a government student ought to do better, but as I can not yet teach in Japanese, and I have no hopes of a position, I have decided to accept for the following month and a half—the summer term.

I do it for practice, and for the good it will do to me to mingle with Japanese girls, and learn their ways and dispositions, and because I feel as if I must work, and not laze at home, and such work would make me feel better, and not give me too much time to worry. Besides, I am sure to like the teaching, which will be easy—some geography or history or English conversation. To be sure, it will take much of my time as Tsukiji, the foreign district, is an hour's ride from here, to go in all weathers. And they want me at the school, from one until four on Mondays, Tuesdays, Wednesdays and Thursdays—taking a good slice in the day, and then the pay is not very much, though good for Japan, 20 yen a month—about $15—but five yen go for jinricksha fares. Still . . . taking all and all . . . I have just sent an answer accepting finally. Now are you not surprised that I am going to be a school ma'am right away, and teach the little Japanese? Father is very willing to have me teach, as I told him I wanted to be getting experience before the government calls on me, or in case, in the remote future, I may have a school of my own somewhere, and though it seems almost an impossibility, who knows but what I might. . . . Hurrah! for the first beginning, though so little. It will seem very funny to hear lessons and order the children and keep quiet, and really and truly earn money. Why, I feel like a child and a schoolgirl myself, and really I am only eighteen. All the other teachers are old; most of them will never see thirty again.

INDIGNATION

Six months had passed since Umeko's return to Japan, and she began to teach at a Methodist school through an introduction by Shige. It was a first-time experience for Umeko. For six weeks in June and July, four days a week from one in the afternoon till four, she taught different subjects to several groups in the same classroom. In a letter to Adeline she explained that she taught two pupils the alphabet, history to another two, grammar, geography and English conversation to eight others, and reading and spelling to five.

June 6, 1883

> The lessons are all easy, but still I have to talk and explain very much, for these girls don't always understand, but they do try so hard, and in anything like memorizing they are quick as a flash.

No doubt she taught different subjects to the groups to accommodate their varying levels of English. That is how children of diverse ages were instructed at *terakoya*, so-called "temple schools" of the Edo period, and also in America, where in those days and even today, the traditional guiding principle of education is to teach students in accordance with their ability.

I taught the Japanese language for a time at a school in the U.S.[1] and everyone at the school seemed to take it for granted that children should be treated differently according to their scholastic aptitude. I think there were six to eight classes in each grade at the school where I taught, with twenty to twenty-five children per class. The classes were ranked by scholastic

---

1　At Baranof Elementary School in Sitka, Alaska, in the late 1960s.

performance, beginning with Class A, and only Class A had lessons in Japanese. Japanese was treated as a foreign language just like French or Spanish, and lessons were provided from first grade through twelfth grade.

In one sense, the children were not being given an equal opportunity. However, most Americans seemed to accept this approach, and at the root of the shared consensus was the idea that it was natural for people to be treated differently according to their ability. This was not merely a matter of dividing pupils into classes on the basis of their grades. Even in the same class, a diligent and competent teacher was expected to break the children up into five groups, for example, and give each group different tasks to do, or different types of homework. I was not particularly diligent and had some reservations about the method, so I taught all of Class A together. But after I had taught them for several years, the gap between those who thrived and those who lost interest grew fairly wide, and because a subject like Japanese depends somewhat of a knack for languages, and because children differ in their aptitude for literature and other such things, I came up against the difficulty of respecting individuality within the one large class. I am not particularly gifted as an educator, but I do feel strongly that human connections such as love and mutual trust, which are born only through personal contact between teacher and student, are an important aspect of education. It even made me think that individual tutoring might be the best type of education. I obsessed about loving each child equally. But the children were so different in temperament and it was very difficult and exhausting to treat them all equally when there were so many of them.

I lived in a dormitory from the time I was in secondary girls' school before and during the war, and during my four years at Tsuda College, so I spent my days in and out of the classroom with people of all ages, both older and younger than me, and I believe that children learn a great deal from each other. My own experience taught me that students learn more from being in intimate groups where people of different ages, temperaments and talents mix and mingle, rather than being exclusively in one-on-one relationships. I think that humans must have survived as a species by living in groups, while simultaneously expressing their own individuality and also recognizing the individuality of others.

In any event, Umeko's first teaching experience would have been a valuable experience for the future educator. School finished in mid-July, and Umeko, free of her duties, sent Adeline a present purchased with part of the thirty yen she had earned.

July 15, 1883

... they were bought with the money I myself, truly, earned—thirty yen in all it was and more than seven went to jinriksha man, and I got mother something with a little of it, and got a trifle for myself and payed my Japanese teacher—and I have a little left, that I think I may buy myself some silk, and have it made up, but I have not decided yet. I think a dark silk, good for any season will come in very nicely, for I need it, I think very much.

Summer vacation began and two foreign missionaries invited Umeko to climb Mount Fuji with them. It was an unusual thing for a Japanese woman to do in those days, but she traveled by jinriksha, sedan chair, and boat, walked a good deal, stayed overnight in ramshackle country inns and rude mountain huts, visited the hot springs in Hakone, and crossed over to the island of Enoshima during her first long journey in Japan.

The Fuji climb was attended by coolies, but Umeko and her two companions (a man and a woman) climbed a steep ascent of eight miles and walked more than ten miles on a more level path, so one can see that she was a good walker. The entire trip took about one week. Her account of the journey is fascinating in its minute description of the manners of the time.

August 2, 1883

. . . It was a very expensive trip for such a short time, and going with foreigners, I had to stay where they did, and that would be at the most expensive, and then the coolies who carry the luggage single out foreigners to cheat and impose, and exact three times as much as from Japanese. The sight of a foreign dress even makes prices go up, and so I had to pay dear for going with foreigners, but still it was pleasant. Of course, we none of us knew much of the language, and I had to use it a great deal at the inns, because my friend Miss Spencer knew nothing at all. Such inconveniences, too, we had to put up with, having only screens and curtains to dress by sometimes, and one room which we divided off to sleep in. Travelling, too, in Japan is very hard—no steam cars and express wagons, etc.—but all the luggage is carried on the shoulders of the coolies, and we ourselves are carried in such funny vehicles into which we have to creep, and sit tailor-fashion all cramped up, or else walk. These vehicles, or *kagos* as they are called, are carried on the shoulders of two men, and they take you everywhere and anywhere, but they are very sharp, and it is hard not to have them cheat you in making all the bargains. Sometimes they get exorbitant when they know you can't get anyone else but themselves. They are so low and ignorant.

Their costume, to say the least, is cool, for it only consists of strips of cloth around their waists. We had to have six or seven with us a good part of the way, though we walked some, and going up Fuji we had four—from the village at the very foot of the mountain to the top is twenty miles, a part of which is comparatively level rising only a few degrees, but the upper part is inclined about forty-five degrees from the perpendicular. An awfully steep road, you may believe. For four miles one may ride, but after that no one can ride a step, nor is any vehicle allowed to pass the gate, because Fuji being sacred, pilgrimages must be on foot—so we had to walk sixteen miles on such an incline as I told you about. For four or five miles the road is good, and beautiful trees and flowers and woods are all around—wood strawberries and cherries, and such pretty ferns. . . . After leaving the pretty walk, one begins to reach the great lava stones, and a rough road. We walked eight miles that day on it. At first one sees great bushes, all around, of trees, but gradually there is nothing but stones and soft lava sand, and a more wild and dreary place one can not easily imagine. We had plenty of clouds all around and about us and saw a thunder storm on one side. We spent the night at the sixth station up, and there are ten in all, and two miles between each. The station is a rude hut [made] out of stones. One sleeps on the bare wood with a sort of mattress spread out on it. All huddled together anyway, coolies in one corner, the men in another, and the women in another, freezing, and dead tired, and the smoke from the wood fire burning right in the room without a chimney. Well, that was roughing it. All the water obtainable was the melted snow, and we paid several cents for a glass. Luckily, my friends had lots of food and I ate that, for on the mountain there is so little indeed. And in walking, we had to take so often brandy and beef tea, and strengthening things.

The day after, we went to the top, starting at daybreak, and reached the foot by evening. Very often I had two coolies to help me, one to push me, and one to pull me by my cane, and in places we had to put down everything, and clamber over the rocks hands and feet, from which a fall would send us rolling at such a speed that we could not stop ourselves. The crater is a wonderful place. The whole dreariness of the mountain takes away the feeling which one has when looking at it from Tokio. It looks so smooth and soft and pretty. Coming down the mountain was fun but quite risky—putting one foot down we would sink almost to shoe top in the soft sand and gravel and on that we would slide forward a foot or two and the next foot would go as far. It was like being on ice, except that the dust flew up into our clothes and cut our faces. I put my hand on the coolie, which helped me. The way the rocks sometimes rolled after us was truly alarming—and, I acknowledge, dangerous. Fuji once in a lifetime is enough.

Coming home, we came a different route from the going. We stopped at Hakone traversing a pretty lake right in the hills by night. Hakone is a great summer resort for foreigners and the mountains around are lovely. We then went to Atami, where the natural hot salt-water geysers are. The water spouts out at a certain time of the tide, and no one can explain it. Some foreigners say that it is one of the most remarkable things in the world. Right by the ocean, all around the geysers spring up bringing boiling hot water. Supposing the water comes by an underground passage, where does it get heated?

We had the benefit of the baths there and at another place where we stopped—such delicious baths, you have no idea, always flowing in and out of a great tub, and you can get in lengthwise, or get out on the floor and scrub, and feel so good afterwards. From Atami we took a boat across the bay to Enoshima, a little island famous for its temples, its caves, and its scenery, and would you believe it, we were all seasick as we could be. . . .

Umeko gives a vivid account of her wide-eyed encounter with Japan's exotic landscape. Her detailed description of the climb up Mount Fuji makes me think that things must be like this today when Japanese go climbing in the Himalayas or South America or Africa, where nothing can be done without the help of locals.

In any case, during this trip, Umeko's Japanese may still have been rudimentary, but she was somehow able to act as interpreter for her foreign friends. She was, nevertheless, treated as a foreigner by the local Japanese and sometimes even asked for her passport.

At the same time, Umeko worried that her English was deteriorating and made a conscious effort to write in that language. During this period she wrote to Adeline every other day, the letters ranging in length from several pages to as many as ten.

Her father Sen visited the Korean Peninsula around the same time at the suggestion of his many Korean friends in Tokyo, and with an invitation from the Korean government. The trip appears to have been related to his work in new Western farming methods. Sen's account of his Korean tour and Umeko's account of her trip in Japan were both sent to Mr. Lanman and published in American magazines under fictional names. Charles Lanman had a high regard for Umeko's writing and probably sold them to a magazine for her, to provide her with extra income. With regard to the Fuji piece, Umeko sent a version that included descriptions of her friends and herself to make the story more interesting, although the names and situations of the people were changed.

> . . . I wanted not to write myself down as either a man or woman, for a Japanese woman who wrote that, it would not be hard to guess who. You may laugh at me for minding people here, but somehow everyone, both Japanese and foreigners, want to know always how we three girls take everything, life, and customs and ways, and they would criticize my criticisms and my language, etc.[2]

Such wariness characterized Umeko throughout her life. Later, when she established her school, she was excessively careful of her language and behavior, and seemed to think that conventional demeanor and avoiding

---

2   From a letter dated September 19, 1883.

public censure were indispensable in achieving a project and vision that were bold and revolutionary.

> I was just then thinking if I could earn ten or twenty dollars on this, that has been a pleasure to write, how nice it would be, and then you could spend five of it, about, for me in little things . . . [that] I don't need, but are nice to have, so high here, and pleasant to get from earnings in America. . . . Is it not good to pay for one's own honest work? I felt it so, when the few yen that was my pay for my month's hard teaching was placed in my hands. Never did money seem so valuable and precious as that little bit, and I felt so proud, and if by writing I could get something, why, that is better still, but I am not sanguine. I would like to buy for Shige a solid silver little spoon, if I could, and if I do earn anything, you buy it for me, not an expensive one. How much are they anyway—about three dollars or more? She has been very kind and had me constantly at her house so I would love to give her something nice.[3]

The money mentioned here is the payment for Umeko's six weeks of teaching at the mission school. Her remarks in an earlier letter reveal reproachful feelings towards the missionaries, for whom Umeko has some blistering words of condemnation:

September 3, 1883

> Last week, I received a letter from one of the teachers of the school, asking me to renew the engagement and teach for them this year if I could. I thought over the subject a great deal . . . and asked if I

---

3   Ibid.

engage to teach, could it be for a shorter time than a whole year—that is, not bind myself to any time in case I should get other work. The answer was they would take me for as long as I could come, the hours, the pay, and the work to be the same. Well, I had to think and think . . . and so I almost decided to—but then I thought of the long, long ride, the hurry, and the getting off in any and every weather of the winter, the steady teaching in the best hours of the afternoon, keeping me from any entertainment or recreation, for about fifteen yen net a month, and thought for my own self it would certainly not pay. Then day after day of such steady work would tire me so, and I would surely neglect my Japanese from sheer want of time, and I would have little time for myself or my clothes, or anything, so as Father is not home, with the advice of the others, after talking it over I wrote and refused saying the work with my study and all would be too much for me, and I am sure it is true, for such mean pay—even Mr. Soper said last summer, when I was, so to speak, on trial, "You are doing missionary work, for the pay is not much." Oh, the missionaries make me so mad, that were I in America, and felt that all the missionaries were like these, not a cent of mine should go for missions. Here in Japan where living is so cheap, food and labor so abundant, the missionaries revel in luxury, far better than at home. They may say in justification that their salaries are not so much, but it buys much. Why, then, are the schools so poor, food so miserable to the working and growing boys and girls, that it is only fit for the lower classes? Why, then, instead of giving themselves more than three courses and a dessert, don't they take care of their scholars? Are we so far below them that their common sense, religion, and charity can not reach us? In my brother's school run by the Methodist mission, are buildings, one with dormitories for one hundred and fifty boys, recitation, dining, and school rooms, and everything for them. There are, besides, houses, separate, for the teachers, three in all, for about five families. One of these latter, costs more than the whole thing for all the scholars. The whole thing is put together and accounted in America, but almost all of it goes to giving the teachers elegant dwellings, high ceilings, porches, balconies, and every kind of comfort. Are their consciences, so tender in talking religion, and dis- tributing tracts, hard on this? Are they blind? I am not, and it makes me indignant, so that I feel at times, away with the whole lot of them, exceptions and all!! Away with the [foreign] missionaries, professors, advisers, lawyers, teachers, [and] let Japan go in ignorance and hon- esty!! In my calmer moments, I must reconsider, and try and make all allowances. But these ladies, who I am dealing with, offer me a paltry sum. One of them has gone home, and I am wanted for her place. She had her room there, and, of course, there was the household expenses to take out, that I have not, still she was not obliged to go the ride and pay for it every day. At the very least, as I know, she got fifty dollars a month and perhaps as high as seventy-five dollars, yet they want me to teach for something about fifteen dollars—twenty yen, five being for fare—and I have the exact same work as she. Either the mission or the people make off [with] the difference. The thought of this, and of the hard work, made me decide, and I sent a refusal. Please don't let people know what I say about all this, but sometime you can tell Mr. Lindsey how I feel, and about my brother's school costing so little, a single family's dwelling so much, and tell him all this which Japanese feel. I don't say that there are not some very honorable exceptions to all this, but somehow, it weakens my faith in human nature terribly, though I do like some of these people very much socially.

I can almost feel the heat of Umeko's indignation. Her writing is at its best when she scribbles something all at once in a fit of passion, but even then, she is careful of detail and maintains her balance with a measure of reasonableness and intelligence. It is no wonder that Charles Lanman thought her writing good enough to be marketed in America.

Umeko was critical of the missionaries in Japan, but found peace in her Christian God, writing in another letter to Adeline that it is no doubt because they were in God's great hands that they could remain in contact as they did. There were times when she felt an absence of His grace, but she felt comfort in placing herself in His hands and that the world would be an empty place indeed if she were ever to lose her faith and become an atheist.

Umeko sent Adeline a small present, had a photo taken of herself in a jinriksha and enclosed it in a letter, and shared girlish gossip with her about Sutematsu's wedding preparations. She reacted naively and with no fuss to the things and events of her daily life, and meanwhile hardened her resolve to save the women of her native land by different means than Sutematsu, although they would work together in some ways.

Umeko's letters are full of detailed descriptions that bring to life the state of affairs in Japan during that era. Letters like hers must have been a rarity in those days, as Umeko aptly notes in her criticism of Japanese letter writing in general.

August 28, 1883

. . . The Japanese system of letter writing is never used to communicate words, thoughts, and actions as if in conversation, exchanging thought for thought. Great men in literature or intimate friends never write and write such long letters that tell all the minutiae of everyday life—the letter writing style is so formal, it does not admit of it. It is only used to tell some important thing, to congratulate, to announce birth, death, or marriage, for business, for especial reason, or to occasionally let different families hear how they get along.

Husbands and wives write to tell each other how they are, but they don't tell everything that they would talk about. Hence to Japanese, the desultory, friendly correspondence to be kept up constantly is very hard, and even, we, who write in English, get affected by it, and feel lazy about writing. This is the chief reason that Japanese don't write to you. I don't suppose it is possible to judge of a Japanese scholar about his life and mind simply from his letters; there are no such books as letters telling opinions, and criticisms, and showing the character distinctly.

I am sure that many people think that Japanese letter writing is still very much the same, but let me add that most Japanese—aside from people like Umeko—will talk casually about mundane matters in conversation, but are conditioned to avoid expressing any personal opinions they might have. This makes it exceedingly difficult to judge a person's view of life, principles, or heart, either from a letter or from a conversation.

To "split one's gut and talk" is a typical Japanese term. Smart people do not go about showing the contents of their guts, and conversely, a fool is an insensitive person who cannot read other people's guts without being told. Being "intelligent" is code for "having imagination" not only in Japan but all over the world, I think, but the value placed on the ability to express one's own thoughts would seem to be another matter. That is, Japan has a different standard with regard to self-expression, and it is a standard that places value on silence. In a way, when a shared aesthetic roots itself too firmly among a group of people, they lose their sensitivity to other ways of thinking and feeling and the result is an unfortunate lack of imagination.

When different cultures mix, on the other hand, the imagination expands in breadth, grows richer, leaps upward. Umeko makes another observation regarding Japanese society:

August 12, 1883

... Japanese don't do much visiting. If anyone wants to meet Japanese, he must meet them in their own homes, must know language and customs, and be able without turning up his nose to conform a little, at least, to our ways. Of course, Japanese do not go out of their way to meet foreigners, especially as they have been so cheated by so many of them, and there is a feeling against the whole lot of them. In order to overcome prejudice, one must be cautious and discreet.

This seems to be in answer to a request from Adeline asking Umeko to introduce an American visitor to Japan to someone with influence. Very few of Adeline's letters remain in comparison to the great volume of those by Umeko, so we can only guess at their contents. However, Adeline appears to have been an equally diligent correspondent.

Adeline writes mostly about common friends and acquaintances in America in the surviving letters. She shows a blend of motherly feeling and the affection of a friend and equal; she is always concerned for Umeko's health and lends a serious ear to her personal concerns.

Tokugawa Iesato's birth mother was the elder sister of Umeko's mother, so Umeko sometimes visited the palace where she lived. Iesato, Umeko's cousin, had studied abroad, so she no doubt looked forward to talking with him as well.

September 17, 1883

... This evening I have just come from the palace, where we went to call, and found there the young lord, who was in England, also making a visit. He talked to me in English, and I felt more at home, though the more I see this small palace life, the more I think of the ridiculousness and difficulty of my ever going near the Imperial court. These palace people are so narrow-minded, so unwilling to move out of their small grooves, so particular in their own peculiar notions, so little educated, except in their own ceremonies, in fact know so little of the world, that to be always with them and doing their ways would be very hard. No court for me! I feel sorry for the young prince from England—so full is his life of forms and ceremonies, and he must keep up the dignity of his rank, and do just so. I know he longs once in a while to relax and do anything unconventionally. I believe he dislikes it, and he will go away soon. . . . In all that form and ceremony it is a wonder any children can grow up, and they do die almost as soon as they are born. You know, perhaps, that Japan has been in mourning the past week for two of her princesses, but after all they were only girls. . . . Now of all the many, only one of this generation is left, the heir apparent, and if he should die, what a mourning there would be!

Meanwhile, Yamakawa Sutematsu was busy organizing and preparing for her marriage to Ōyama Iwao in the fall and was rather enjoying the arrangement of her lavish trousseau. Evening gown, wedding gown, a dress for receptions, a morning dress and afternoon dress. Western-style clothing, Japanese-style kimonos, visiting dresses, party dresses, undergarments, lace, furniture, and household goods. The more she heard, the less interested Umeko became in marriage for herself.

How did Umeko feel toward Sutematsu, who would be a noble lady in the class-based society of the age and no longer permitted to associate with commoners? Watching her friend blithely preparing for the future that had unexpectedly dropped into her lap, Umeko, herself of marriageable age, must have felt a twinge of jealousy. But she also knew that Sutematsu was losing something in return, so she probably had mixed feelings about the whole affair.

In a letter dated May 13, 1883, she wrote:

> I saw Shige lately, and she says Stematz is looking so badly and so thin. I am much worried about it. I don't know whether it is the change of climate and food, or else the taking care of her mother who has been quite ill, and her sister-in-law who is sick too. Poor Steam's hands are truly busy, and she helps to keep house too. I am so sorry for her. I think she truly needs our friendship and love so much. And what will her future be I wonder . . .

Umeko gave careful thought to what she should give Sutematsu for a wedding present and appears to have settled on a bolt of fine, white, twilled silk that could be made into a dress. In answer to Adeline's query as to what she ought to send, Umeko answered that a dress would be nice, but that if Adeline intended to send one to Sutematsu, she should send one to Shige too, as it was better not to make the smallest distinction between the two. Shige was already married, but Adeline could say that she had not been able to send anything in time for the wedding. So she should either send something to both, or to neither, which was also fine.

Here, too, is the impression that she regarded Sutematsu's impending marriage with a somewhat cool eye. The more lavish the preparations, the more the feeling of being abandoned by someone she thought had shared her dreams, and this made her own determination all the stronger.

One reason that Umeko did not aspire to marriage like her two friends was the presence of her father. Sen was a progressive thinker with Western leanings, and the whole family was influenced by his thinking. As she frequently wrote in her letters, no one pressured Umeko to behave by the normal standards of Japanese womanhood. In fact, her family may have hoped that she would live the life of an entirely new kind of woman, if that was what she wanted. Why else would they have sent a seven-year-old child to live in a strange land for eleven years?

Tsuda Sen's work in Western-style agriculture was fashionable for a time, but his popularity soon waned, according to Umeko's letters. He had a large family to support and suffered financial problems, but never to the point that their livelihood was endangered. His *Nōgyō zasshi* (Agriculture Magazine) was launched in 1876 and remained in publication for more than forty years. Sen envisioned agriculture as a business undertaking in the framework of a liberal economy, but Japanese agriculture did not shed its feudal underpinnings for many years and never quite developed in the way he hoped.

CHAPTER

6

INVITATION

Roughly a year after her return to Japan, a gentleman came up to Umeko at a ball given by Foreign Minister Inoue at his official residence on the occasion of the Emperor's birthday (November 3). The gentleman smiled at her affectionately and turned out to be Itō Hirobumi, who had been on the same ship as the seven-year-old Umeko twelve years earlier as a vice-envoy of the Iwakura Mission.[1]

November 5, 1883

. . . It is said that out of the invitations issued, one thousand were accepted, so you can imagine something of the crowd; at the same time it was very select, and only those well known were asked. Mr. and Mrs. Inoue, of course, received the guests. It is the first time that I have seen the full court dress of the officials, all the court decorations and gold lace. Gold lace abounded on every side—navy officers, officials, etc. The ladies' dresses, too, were very beautiful . . . What seemed interesting especially was the dress of the court ladies, of whom there were several, in the regular, old Japanese court fashion, very curious and very beautiful. The Chinese minister's wife was there also, in her party dress, and lots and lots of curious folk. Although the house was very roomy, and all thrown open, at times the crowd seemed so great, and though one might see a friend there, perhaps for three

---

1   When Umeko was sent to America in 1871, she and the other girls were part of a large diplomatic mission dispatched to the U.S. and Europe by the Japanese government. Iwakura Tomomi led the mission in the role of plenipotentiary ambassador, and the 100-strong group included three government ministers (including Itō Hirobumi), numerous administrators, scholars, students, and attendants. One of the initial goals of the mission was to renegotiate treaties with Western countries; another was to observe and learn from the West. The former was not achieved, but the latter had a long-reaching effect on the development of modern Japan.

hours you might not come across him again. There was dancing, but it was almost impossible to dance. In the meantime, outside, the most beautiful fireworks were being fired, of all kinds and sorts. I got a little look at them, but it was too cold to stand outside. The most beautiful fireworks were the stars, which seemed most brilliant on this night.

. . . Another one who came to me and made me feel embarrassed was Mr. Ito. He came and said to me, "Do you remember me?" and I looked and could not call him to mind at all, and after a little while in which I felt dreadful, he said, "I am Ito," and then I remembered. He is such a great man now, that I could not but feel embarrassed when he asked if I had forgotten him.

The image of the five girls in their long-sleeved kimonos, traveling to America to be educated, must have been firmly etched in the memories of Itō and others of the Iwakura Mission, and Itō had no doubt heard that Tsuda Umeko, youngest of the five, was back in Japan after eleven years of study. From March 1882 to August 1883, Itō himself had been in Europe to study the constitutions of various countries, and he was now back in Japan to draft the Meiji Constitution.

Umeko had only a vague recollection of their acquaintance twelve years earlier, but it must have been a profound moment for Itō, to encounter the little girl who had matured into a young woman during the revolutionary decade that brought him to his present position. That same evening, he introduced Umeko to a woman named Shimoda Utako.

A few days later, Itō asked Umeko's father, Tsuda Sen, to come and see him, and told him that he wanted to invite Umeko to stay in his home as a live-in guest, in order that she might tutor his wife and daughter in the English language and Western manners, and to perform the duties of an interpreter. With the Rokumeikan[2] due to open shortly on November 28, Itō had no doubt been mulling over the problem of how Japanese women should mix socially with Westerners at official functions, and also considering the education of his own wife and daughter.

The brief exchange with Umeko on the night of the ball and the impression it left on him no doubt led to his invitation. Another factor might have been her close friendship with Sutematsu, whose husband Ōyama Iwao was minister of the army. Itō was a native of Chōshu, while Ōyama came from Satsuma,[3] and Ōyama had married Sutematsu, whereas he himself was married to a former geisha. There might have been an element of rivalry in his approach to Umeko.

Itō introduced Umeko to Shimoda Utako on November 3 and soon mediated plans for them to exchange lessons in Japanese and English, and for Umeko to teach English at Tōyō Girls' School, where Shimoda was principal. The initial plan was for Umeko to commute from home to teach school in the mornings and afternoons, and to take lunch with the Itōs in between. But this would not give them sufficient time, so it was decided that she would live in their home, not as a hired tutor, but as a guest and friend.

Shortly before the year's end, Umeko moved into the official residence in Nagata-chō where Itō lived with his family. She spent Sundays with her own family in Azabu, where she decorated a Christmas tree and invited Itō's daughter to come and see it. Umeko describes Itō and his family in a letter written to Adeline during the New Year's holiday of 1884:

---

2 A large Western-style guesthouse built in Hibiya, near the Imperial Palace, to impress foreign dignitaries and to familiarize the Japanese with Western customs. Elaborate balls and banquets took place there and it became a byword for Westernization, but it was also controversial and was no longer used for such purposes after 1890.

3 There was a longstanding rivalry between the feudal domains of Chōshu and Satsuma that supposedly went back to the Battle of Sekigahara in 1600. The two factions overcame their differences to form an uneasy alliance that brought the Meiji government into power, and they dominated politics well into the twentieth century. They never quite trusted each other, however, and often competed for power.

January 4, 1884

. . . They are, indeed, very kind to me and always treat me with honor, nay almost respect, in spite of my awful Japanese, broken and rude as it is. I can't realize my life here. It is so strange. Just imagine living in a house guarded by policemen at all gates, and going about so. It is a very luxurious life here. I hope it won't spoil me. Our meals even are very fine. At dinner our usual course is first soup, then fish, followed by two kinds of meats with vegetables, then dessert, and after that, fruit. In the morning, as is the foreign custom in Japan, there is very little—only two courses, and at lunch we have Japanese food. You can see that they live very richly. Of course, it seems a great deal to me.

Now I must tell you about my grand dinner party. I told you that Mr. Ito was going to give one to the ministers and diplomats, and he told me to go, so I did and stood with Mrs. Ito to receive her guests and did translate a wee bit for her. I was introduced as her friend and translator, and though I felt awkward, and as if I didn't belong there, Mr. and Mrs. Ito were very kind. It was a grand dinner and about thirty were present, and I was the only one of so little account. . . .

Mr. Ito and I have had some very serious talks on all sorts of subjects. He seems very anxious to promote the interest of Japan in every way—socially, morally, politically, intellectually. He is anxious to establish a school and to have me learn Japanese. Sometimes when I tell him about many things, about books, or interesting things about women's work, he tells me I must tell Japanese ladies all these sorts of things—about work and taking care of the sick, and the worth of knowledge, etc. He wants me to learn and to bring me forward so that I can, and he is very kind. It was, however, only last night that he began to ask me about Christianity and we talked nearly two hours on it. He is in favor of it, acknowledged that its morals and teachings surpassed that of any other religion and that for Japan, Christianity would be a good thing. Still, he by no means believes at all. Only he says it is good. Then he told me about his travels in Europe and all. And finally he mentioned that he knew but little of Christianity, he should like to hear more of it, and all its beliefs. Now imagine how I feel. What grand possiblities [sic] are here! What can I say or do? Even of last night I have thought of much I might have said and did not. I am so ignorant I can hardly give reasons for my own belief, much less argue or persuade. I only know I do believe. If I could say anything to put in the right any question asked me, how glad I would be! How splendid if Christianity would find a hold here. Mr. Ito is of no religion, neither Buddhist, nor Shintoist. . . . I often think of the Bible verse which I think is like this: "Take no heed what ye shall say, for it shall be given unto thee what ye shall say. For it is not ye that speak but the Father in thee." So if any chance occurs I pray that it may not be lost and each day its seed may be cast not for evil but for good. There is no doubt that Mr. Ito is interested in Christianity and thinks it is very good in many ways. . . . Anyhow my religion is not opposed here and it is very good to hear any beginnings. But that he even takes an interest in it can not be openly said in Japan, nor would he acknowledge it, I think. It is very early, indeed. I only tell you to interest you, between ourselves. I found, very much to my surprise, that one of the attendants here is also a Christian. He told me so, and that he was also only lately baptized, and all about it. So I have another fellow Christian under the same roof. Is it not strange?

I am myself without religion and find it difficult to write about Umeko and Christianity. But I realize that Christianity is a very important element of her character and want to be as fair as possible in describing her attitude to religion. As previously recounted, Umeko was clear-sighted about the missionaries who were in Japan at the time, and she herself was never fanatical about anything. Twelve years earlier when the five young students left Japan, Christianity was still officially banned and the girls were given a list of instructions for overseas travelers that included the words: "It is strictly forbidden to acquire foreign citizenship or to undergo a religious conversion."[4]

Nevertheless, Umeko was baptized during her third year in America, in 1873, at the Old Swedes' Church in Philadelphia. Yoshikawa Toshikazu writes in *Tsuda Umeko den* (Biography of Tsuda Umeko) that she was baptized of her own will, but I think that a nine-year-old child who was sent to Sunday school every week and lived among Christians in American society was bound to accept the Christian faith as a way of life. Yoshikawa's biography notes that the Lanmans were members of the Episcopal Church, but they were flexible and also attended services of the Presbyterian Church. Thinking it best for Umeko to belong to a non-denominational church, they had her baptized at Old Swedes' (properly Christ Church, Upper Merion).[5]

Mori Arinori, chargé d'affaires in the U.S. at the time, was also consulted in the matter. The prohibition of Christianity had officially come to an end in Japan in February 1873, and marriage to a foreigner became permissible in March. Times were changing, so the adults in charge of Umeko considered her character and feelings, and acted accordingly.

In any case, the Lanmans were liberal-minded intellectuals who made no deliberate or forceful attempt to convert the child who had been entrusted to their care. This attitude is evident in the letters they wrote regularly to Tsuda Sen in Japan. They believed that education was a matter of respecting the free choice of the student, who should not be forced by circumstances to do anything. They were, in fact, careful to nurture the spontaneous development of Umeko's young mind.

---

4   Yoshikawa, *Tsuda Umeko den*, 45.
5   Ibid., 91–95.

It seems to me that this attitude, firmly embedded in Umeko's spirit as a legacy from her foster parents, was in evidence when she later established her own school. Umeko was a pious Christian who believed in God, and as an educator, she judged that it would be a good thing to train the minds of the new Japan on the basis of Christian values.

Umeko grew to adulthood in the Christian world of late nineteenth century America, and she must have compared the women of her native country—who lived by the precepts of Confucian morality and the worldview of East Asian Buddhism—to women in Western society and felt that there was no choice in the matter. The prevalent social mores of the day thought nothing of a man having both wife and mistress(es), and this was unacceptable from a woman's point of view, particularly for a woman who had grown up under Christian morality.

Another point is, as Umeko herself mentions from time to time in her letters, that Christianity in Japan was not a religion of the wealthy or ruling classes up to this time, but rather of the poor and oppressed, as is evidenced in the history of persecuted Christians. Christianity was no longer prohibited when Umeko returned and several mission schools had been established, and it was from this period that Christianity began to answer not only the yearning of the poor and oppressed for practical deliverance, but the desire of the educated classes for intellectual release.

Tsuda Sen turned to Christianity after a trip to Austria with Sano Tsunetami and others for the 1873 Vienna World Exposition. In 1875, he and his wife had themselves baptized by Reverend Soper[6] and he enrolled his son in a Methodist school. Sen dedicated his life to Western-style agriculture, establishing a school for agriculture, launching an agricultural magazine, devising various farming tools, and managing a farm of his own.

---

6   Julius Soper (1845–1937), an American Methodist missionary active in Japan in the late 1800s.

Umeko's letter shows her in an evangelical mood, but her criticism of missionaries in Japan, as recounted in the previous chapters, also reveals her to be a level-headed observer of people of religion. Throughout her life, her greatest concern was to honor human life and expand its visions.

In the same letter, she describes the changes she saw in Sutemetsu:

> ... You will be sorry if I tell you that Sutematsu never goes to church, and seems to have forgotten her profession. She seems so submissive to Mr. Oyama, that though he would not forbid her going, still as he doesn't go, she doesn't venture, especially as Sunday is his day home. I do not have patience with such wifely tameness. She goes to the extreme of Japanese custom. Still it may be that it is because the honeymoon is hardly over and it won't last. She is too submissive, and seems to have lost her will. I am very sorry. She seems to have gone back, and I am sure she never begins to keep Sunday, and dinner parties and all keep on all the same because Mr. Oyama goes, and she doesn't even say she doesn't want to do it. Maybe she doesn't care anyhow. I feel very sorry about it. And Sutematsu, too, is getting very artificial in her dress and looks. It is too bad. All to please Mr. Oyama, I suppose.

This report brings home to me both Umeko's disappointment and Sutematsu's amiable nature. Yes, that's exactly how it must have been, I think. I can see in my mind's eye what the world was like back then.

Reading Umeko's many letters, I am struck by an artless innocence that has a backbone of fine intellect. People who knew her personally unanimously declared that she was never proud or snobbish about her academic accomplishments, despite her fame and superior foreign education. She was a woman with uncommonly luxurious black hair and a well-kept appearance, who held passionately to her ideals. Her young students loved and respected her to the point of adulation.

It was no doubt these aspects of her character that led Itō to invite her into his home. At the same time, the seriousness with which he discussed Japan's future with nineteen-year-old Umeko, a mere girl, show him to be the great politician that he was—the man who tore down many antiquated institutions. He lent Umeko books about American democracy and told her that just as Japan had developed outwardly and materially in the previous twenty years, it would undergo the same kind of development, inwardly, in the next twenty. Young Umeko was thrilled to hear a man's view on such matters, and at such close quarters.

My thoughts turn now to the mood of the world that Itō and other high officials of the Japanese government carried back to Japan from their numerous inspection tours and extended visits to America and Europe. To begin with, the state of America during Umeko's long sojourn: the Civil War had ended a decade earlier and the United States set aside a feudal-type agricultural fundamentalism in favor of modern capitalism. It was a new and growing nation, bursting with the pioneer spirit of the New World, and it was a hodge-podge of Puritanism, materialism, and non-conformism, all in one melting pot. A strange, novel, multiethnic and multiracial world was emerging. In one sense, it was a land of rebels, dreamers, have-nots and paupers driven out of old Europe and come to America in search of fresh beginnings. Japanese students must have landed in this newborn land of boundless promise and seen infinite visions of the future.

If the Japanese archipelago did not lie in the Pacific Ocean, and if the advanced Western countries of the time were limited to old Europe and did not include the United States of America, Japan's history might have been different. Or we could just say that the Meiji Restoration was what it was because the contortions of the world were what they were at the time.

Mr. and Mrs. Lanman, Umeko's foster parents, were contemporaries of American intellectuals such as Emerson, Thoreau, Whitman, Hawthorne, Melville, Longfellow, and Irving. The couple were personally acquainted with a number of these men and Umeko had met some of them. They were poets and philosophers born of the vast natural wilderness of the New World.

Europe, on the other hand, was the ancestral land of the people who established the New World and eventually claimed their independence from the old. The Old World was languishing in a fin-de-siècle fit of melancholy and torpor that expressed itself as decadence and aestheticism. In France, the great revolution of 1789 was a thing of the distant past, and Paris—City of Flowers—was now a town of pensioners and bourgeoisie, prostitutes, homosexuals, and laborers. Baudelaire, Mallarmé, Flaubert, Maupassant, Zola and Rimbaud were its voices.

In England, 1888 was the year Jack the Ripper shocked the world with a serial killing of prostitutes. As I write this chapter in August 1989, Japanese television insistently broadcasts the face of the suspect charged with the serial killing of young girls, and my mind ponders the history of the past century. England led the world into the Industrial Revolution and the British Empire ruled the world in the name of colonialism and conservatism. In literature, Stevenson wrote the *Strange Case of Dr. Jekyll and Mr. Hyde* in 1886 and Hardy and Wilde were publishing book after book. Marx, exiled from Germany, was in London trying to finish *Das Kapital*. Nietzsche and Wagner were being productive in Germany and Austria. Freud was analyzing the human psyche, and Mendel was pondering the laws of genetics. In Russia, Dostoyevsky wrote *The Brothers Karamazov* in 1880, Tolstoy penned "Ivan the Fool" in 1885, and Chekhov would write "Ward No. 6" in 1892.

In Japan, Itō Hirobumi, having observed various countries with his own eyes, was drafting the Constitution of the Empire of Japan (better known as the "Meiji Constitution") under the watchful eyes of the nineteen-year-old Umeko. The Dajōkan (Grand Council of State) was abolished, a Cabinet was established in its place, and Itō became Japan's first prime minister in 1885. In the world of literature, Tsubouchi Shōyō published *Shōsetsu shinzui* (The Essence of the Novel) and *Tōsei shosei katagi* (The Character of Modern Students) in 1885 and Futabatei Shimei published *Ukigumo* (Floating Clouds) in 1887.

The Korean Peninsula was in a state of civil war and Qing-dynasty China was under the control of the Empress Dowager Cixi. Indochina was a territory of France.

I wonder if the nineteen-year-old Umeko felt the slow spinning of the world as she watched Itō Hirobumi in his prime, drafting a new constitution for modern Japan. Itō was forty-three years old.

Soon after Umeko moved in with the Itōs, she accompanied Mrs. Itō, her daughters, two servants, and a cook on a lavish journey to Atami. Departing on January 11, they rode in sedan chairs for half the distance and walked the other half, stopping overnight in Odawara and sojourning for three weeks in the specially appointed annex of a hotel. Itō probably arranged the trip so that Mrs. and Miss Itō could continue their English lessons and Umeko could study Japanese. Umeko describes the situation in a letter to Adeline.

Atami
January 13, 1884

The English language study is very hard and rather slow, and I do not think she [Mrs. Ito] is so very quick in learning, but I must try my best, for they do a great deal for me. Of course, they pay everything for me on this trip. The invitation meant that, and according to Japanese custom I must not offer to pay, nor discuss such things with Madam, so I must accept all their bounty, and repay it the best I can, by teaching and by helping where I can, and by being good. They treat me very kindly and speak always politely, and are very formal and ceremonious to me, so that I am like a guest, and feel rather stiff and stilted. Of course, it is nicer to act more free and easy, and more at home, but I can't help that, and it is their way of showing respect and kindness to me, so I must accept it. . . . I shall return their kindness as much as I can by my teaching. . . .

Living with a family not her own, Umeko looked back on her own life and began to see the differences between America and Japan from a different angle. She thought a great deal about children and women, in particular, and looked back wistfully on her childhood with the Lanmans, sheltered and adored. She compared it to her present life, where she was treated with kindness but set apart like an alien presence, held at a respectful distance.

But childhood was childhood, and she couldn't be a child forever. Someone blessed with a special life like hers could surely look forward to a young adulthood full of rewarding experiences, so she would not fret, and she would cherish her memories as she went forward to pursue her dreams. She would never have better friends than Mr. and Mrs. Lanman, but Mr. Itō was a good friend, she wrote, and she repeated how lucky she was to have made such a *great* friend.

In February, Mrs. Itō and her daughters became ill, Mrs. Itō seriously so. Her rheumatism took a bad turn and her face was swollen and badly inflamed. There was an exchange of telegrams with Tokyo and Mr. Itō rushed to Atami, bringing their family doctor. Itō Hirobumi's arrival put the Atami hotel in an uproar, for there was a steady stream of visitors in addition to four policemen and numerous attendants. Depending on the company, Miss Itō, as the daughter of the house, was obliged to wait on the guests in accordance with Japanese custom.

Atami

February 11, 1884

Here I am in Atami yet, delayed by circumstances. We have had an
anxious time since I last sent you a letter, for Mrs. Ito and the child
and Miss Ito have been in turn sick, but Mrs. Ito in especial. She has
had very bad rheumatism, and her face has been all swollen and in a
most fearful, inflamed condition. Telegrams flew back and forth from
Tokio, and three days ago Mr. Ito decided to come on and bring with
him the regular doctor, the best around. After that we were much
relieved, although we had a good doctor here. I have been anxious
indeed for I could not help, nor do much and I feared I was in the
way if I tried to help. . . The weather was fearful, and even in warm
Atami the snow of Tokio, about a foot or two, reached us just to make
it horrid. We kept putting off our departure day after day, and finally
Mrs. Ito grew worse and at last, Mr. Ito and the doctor came very fast
and arrived here two days ago, much to our delight. . . . Since then
Mrs. Ito has gotten better, and today [she] is doing nicely so that we
think we can go back in a few days. . . . Mrs. Ito's face was fearfully
swollen and one eye almost closed and so it was very bad. Miss Ito
was also sick, but it was much lighter and was only trouble[d] with
indigestion, though she was in bed a week, and sick ten days. I have
kept well, but even the servants have been affected by the cold wave
and the very strange unseasonable weather, unusual in Atami. . . .
Of course, Mr. Ito's arrival has made quite a fuss here, as he must
bring with him his four policemen and attendants. Since he arrived
there has been a steady stream of visitors, and now there are some
eight people dining upstairs and Miss Ito has just left me to wait upon
them according to the Japanese custom, which requires it, although
there are dozens of servants that could do it. It is our custom, you

know, and I did at home, though it seems funny for the daughter of a *sangi*, or minister, to be waiting upon the visitors at dinner.

This is a custom that I remember from my own girlhood, and I also recall feeling humiliated and rebelling against it with a "No, I won't!" When I was a girl, the daughter of the house was expected to entertain guests even when there were others to do it. In those days, at a Japanese meal, the wife and daughters of the family did not sit at the table with the guests, but served them from aside.

The custom of women serving has gradually given way to men and women sitting down together—a development no doubt influenced by the introduction of Western manners. Today, since most people do not have servants, it is impossible for a couple to remain seated throughout the meal with their guests, so the usual thing is for the woman to be continually getting up and moving around. In the West, it is common for the host to also move about, but Japanese men are not so mobile. This would seem to be a major reason why Japanese do not entertain casually at home.

It is not the custom in Japan to invite couples together as a unit, but as more and more women work outside the home, it will be interesting to watch how socialization between families develops. Some people think it is easier for both men and women to remain unconcerned about the spouses of workplace colleagues, but in today's world, where both family and community relationships are on the wane, people will make themselves lonelier and lonelier by setting such clear boundaries between home and workplace.

As for the Itōs, when it came time for the family to leave for Tokyo, a large ship sailing up the coast was telegraphed and ordered to make a stop in Atami. In those days, power could be used for such matters. After the ship arrived in Yokohama, the party traveled on to Tokyo by train. Umeko returned to her home in Azabu the next day and she went to see Sutematsu.

While she lived with the Itōs in Nagata-chō, Umeko's custom was to spend Sundays and weekends with her family.

In addition to her room and board in Atami, Itō paid Umeko twenty-five yen, partly for her services in January and partly as a New Year's bonus. This was far more generous than what she had been paid at the Methodist school six months earlier. Mrs. Itō also showered her with gifts for her family when they returned to Tokyo.

All the same, Adeline seems to have written that she was sorry that Umeko should have to work for strangers as a live-in tutor, for Umeko hastened to reassure her in a postscript to a letter dated March 9:

> Surely I am truly blessed all my life. Why do you speak as if you had been anxious. There is nothing to be anxious about. Why spend your time in worry. I knew I must get work and I would get it sometime and I do like my lessons and my scholars very much. I enjoy the work anyway if I need not teach. And I do have a very luxurious time here, in this big elegant house, and many servants and such good times and kind friends and all. Is it not a matter to be congratulated! I am the teacher here, and all respect me. Do you not think it is a position above my years? I think it is and yet I am glad to fill it if I can—Why do you mind? —Rejoice and be glad for me!

Umeko's schedule during her life with the Itōs was as follows: On school days, she rose at seven, dressed in half an hour, then went to the main house to have breakfast with the two Itō daughters. She left for school (where Shimoda Utako was principal) shortly after eight and arrived at nine. She taught English to Shimoda and received a return lesson in calligraphy and Japanese.

After this she taught three classes at the school, a half-hour each, and at twelve o'clock sharp she stopped and returned to the Itō residence. There, she had lunch, gave a lesson to Mrs. Itō and her two daughters, and then had some time for herself, but it was soon time for the evening meal. Dinner was a leisurely affair with a great deal of conversation, followed by more talk around the fire in the parlor. She could read if she returned to her own room, but she sometimes gave an additional lesson in English or some other subject. All in all her schedule was so busy that she sometimes did not have time enough to sew on a missing button, she wrote. After ten, she usually took a bath and sometimes waited up with Mrs. Itō until past midnight for Hirobumi to come home, but Umeko generally went to bed earlier because of her early mornings.

Umeko did not go to the school on Tuesdays, Wednesdays, and Saturdays, so on those days she gave Miss Itō lessons in the morning, and on Wednesdays, she attended a drawing class. (Sutematsu had expressed a desire to learn Japanese drawing, so Itō introduced them to a teacher who arranged a class for them on Wednesdays. They were joined by a young woman from the German legation and a daughter of the American ambassador.)

Among Umeko's students at Tōyō Girls' School were many daughters of the upper classes, including two daughters of Inoue Kaoru, minister of foreign affairs, and a daughter of Nomura Yasushi, who later became minister of communications.

Umeko become acquainted with various powerful political men and other well-known historical figures of the time while she lived with the Itōs. Mori Arinori, who had looked after Umeko during her American years, was now minister of education, and Mrs. Mori requested through Mrs. Itō that Umeko give lessons to her sons—recently returned from England—in geography, spelling, reading, and grammar.

February 28, 1884

Mr. Inoue has returned from his trip and will resume his position of head of the Foreign Department, and so Mr. Ito, then, finishes his term. What changes are to be made in the ministers this spring is not yet settled; Mr. Mori, I believe, is to return home and take some place out here, of honor. With Mr. Yoshida, and Mr. Oyama, and Mr. Ito and Mr. Saigo, I have become acquainted with a good many of the high rank in my one year in [Japan].

Ito established a cabinet system in 1885 and in December became prime minister and minister of the imperial household, thus becoming the most powerful man in Japan, both in name and substance. Umeko felt lucky to be living in the daily presence of this promising new leader, and was proud to be a guest in his household. "Mr. Ito is certainly the most popular man of the day, so I have a *great* friend if I have him. I wonder what will come out of all this, but I can not think nothing will come from it," she wrote in a letter dated May 24, 1884.

Umeko was invited to a party at Rokumeikan and worried about her dress and about her duties as an escort in several of her letters, but for some reason, the description of the ball itself lacks the liveliness that characterizes her other correspondence.

March 7, 1885

Shige has been so kind as to fix up my old white crepe for the ball of the ninth. It looks old-fashioned in this day of wide skirts and bustles, and I did not know what to do with it. Shige told me to bring it to her, and so I did, and while I was at school she fixed it all up, and when I went there, it was all done so nicely. . . . I am expecting to wear that dress tomorrow to the ball, and it looks as well as possible, considering it is old, and somewhat soiled.

March 10, 1885

. . . Father and I went together, and reached Rokumeikan at after nine o'clock. Sutematsu was dressed in yellow brocade which came from China, and she looked very nice.[7] There was a great deal of elegant dressing. . . .

The floor was lovely, the music charming, and all seemed to enjoy it. The supper was a most grand affair, and every luxury loaded the tables. Outside, the grounds were lighted with lanterns, and an electric light, which shone beautifully all around—quite a new thing to many Japanese, and something miraculous to the Corean ambassadors and Chinese diplomats who are here. We did not stay until the end, but it was half past twelve when we left for home, and an hour later before we reached Azabu. It was a clear but bitter cold night for March, and I thought I would freeze, but I did not, very luckily, take cold, and so I congratulate myself on that. I think Sutematsu must have been very tired, for she kept looking around here and there after her many guests, besides standing up two hours, receiving them. Now she will have to receive her party callers for this week.

Of course, coming home so late, I was awfully sleepy this morning, but I had to go to the school, and I could only sleep a little later than usual this morning, so I am very tired tonight, and my feet ache too, and I must go to bed very early. Take it all in all, I am glad I went,

---

7   The ball was hosted by Mr. and Mrs. Ōyama on the occasion of Ōyama's return to Japan, with invitations sent out to 800 guests. Umeko wanted to have a new dress made with some silk she received at New Year's, but there was not enough time.

but it doesn't pay to go very often unless one gives one's whole time to going out. . . .

Needless to say, Sutematsu's letters to Alice Bacon around this time also made frequent mention of Rokumeikan. As would be expected of the young wife of the army minister, she comments on the wives of other important men and voices some criticism of various Japanese and foreign personages, but her tone remains neutral and the letters indicate that she was beginning to make excuses for not attending these affairs.

As for Umeko, a young and single woman, entertainments of this type probably did not impress her with their glamor or strike her as conducive to the realization of her own dreams.

To tell the truth, I had been looking forward to Umeko's reaction to Rokumeikan and searched eagerly for any mention of her impressions, but she almost seemed to avoid any reference to her own feelings. Around the same time, writing about other things, she expressed a clear distaste for the aristocratic hauteur of foreign ambassadors and their wives, with comments to the effect that when she had to be with such people, there was nothing to do but hold up her head and be dignified. I suspect that many of the European ambassadors were of the nobility.

I am reminded of Bigot's famous caricatures of Japanese ladies at a Rokumeikan ball, totally exhausted from an evening in unfamiliar Western dresses and lounging about with backs bent and legs akimbo. Remembering those caricatures, I am also disheartened by the arrogance of the Western artists of the age. They were filled with scorn, without a smidgen of literary sensibility as to the pathos of the Japanese.

In every day and age, powerful nations steal from other nations that are relatively backward. The stolen wealth makes it possible for people of those advanced states to live in luxury as the colonial governors of backward regions. You have only to look at how the Japanese live in countries of the so-called third world today. If a Japanese artist chooses to describe the way people live in such places, the merit of that work over the course of time will depend on the attitude behind the depiction.

European diplomats in Meiji-era Japan may have been nobles, but the nobility of their smirks is somewhat open to question. I am reminded of a painting by the Spanish painter Goya, in which a noblewoman looks into a mirror and a monkey stares back. Not only are the Japanese ladies of Rokumeikan reminiscent of the monkey; so are the Western ladies who looked down their noses at them. It makes me think that the same scene must be taking place in the so-called underdeveloped or backward countries of the world where Japanese are perhaps living like colonial governors.

The popular press in Japan printed many amusing and scandalous stories about the carryings-on of high government officials and their ladies at Rokumeikan, and Itō was a regular target of their interest. His many indiscretions outside the Rokumeikan milieu were well known, and though his wife never permitted any of his mistresses into their home, she is said to have looked after and educated several of the children who resulted from his liaisons. It is hard to say how much Umeko knew of Itō's peccadilloes, but the rumors that reached her ears and the man she saw before her must have posed a perplexing problem to her woman's perception.

January 13, 1884

... Mr. Ito, in spite of his foreign ideas, is far from being moral himself. He stays in the upper foreign house, and I in the Japanese, so *I can't* tell well, but I know *he spends nights out* and no one knows excepting his servants. But Mrs. Ito does not seem to mind very much, for she, of course, knows all about it. It is not considered very bad at all if a man is not too dissipated and has everything in moderation. It is not looked upon with the horror that we are taught to look upon it.

Because only a few years ago it was perfectly lawful and right that such things should be, and every man was expected to have a wife and then some secondary wives. So of course, it is very strange to change so suddenly, and it must be very gradual. . . .

February 26, 1884

It was written in the papers that Mr. Ito and Mr. Inoue spoke most strongly at court against the custom allowing the Emperor to legally have twelve wives, and begged that such things be done away with. That a protestation arises from these men to such an effect is a great thing, though I think that their own lives might be more perfect in some of these ways.

Umeko's comment is delightfully tongue in cheek, straightforward but in a way that tickles the imagination. She is intelligently nonchalant and stays within the bounds of elegance and refinement.

She talked to Mrs. Itō about American customs, let Miss Itō sleep in her room and acted as her confidante, and offered advice about Western clothing, which ordinary people in Japan knew little about. She describes the two women in the following way:

January 20, 1884

. . . Mrs. Ito is a most kind and good mother to her children, and they seem a very happy family, and the little ones obey her most explicitly. The little girl is very, very good, and obedient to a degree that would put many American girls to shame.[8] They are models of politeness and good behavior. It surprises me sometimes to see it. They seem to reverence their father, and his word is law to all, but his faults and his morals seem not to trouble them very much, if it does at all. Alas, too often are such faults passed over, and for the woman, there is no help. . . .

February 23, 1884

. . . She [Miss Ito] is an imperious miss, spoiled a little, and very hard on her servants, very hard to please, and selfish. The maid finds it difficult sometimes to suit her and satisfy her, and she will make all manner of fun of them. She is the eldest daughter and naturally spoiled. Wish I could show her how to be a little more kind often, to those below her, even if she is a little less formal and polite to those above her. The great fault of new democratic nations, that of too great attention to rank, and not to man, reaches even her. It is hard to understand that a beggar's sufferings and bodily sensitiveness are the same as a prince's.

Umeko was surprised at how badly Japanese men behaved when they were intoxicated, and was appalled when Itō came home in a seriously drunken state. She applauded Mrs. Itō's bravery when she rightly scolded him. In those days, American households of the middle class or above apparently took a puritanical and disapproving view of alcohol and insobriety, and Umeko grew up with the idea that drunkenness was a habit of the lower classes.

---

8   Only the eldest daughter was said to be Mrs. Itō's child, but Umeko does not mention this to Adeline.

March 9, 1884

... Mr. Ito had before then been dining out, and had taken plenty of wine, and there he drank plenty, and he really got quite drunk then and Mrs. Ito was so frightened and felt so badly. I knew he does get drunk, but it was the first time that I had seen him in such a way, and I felt very badly about it. I know every one of these great men takes entirely too much very often, and I am sure Mr. Ito felt very sorry afterwards. ... Such things are not treated with the horror they should be, things go on just so. It will take many years and they say that some of them are improving now. I hope they will. ...

In May 1884, Umeko wrote that although Itō spoke with her about Christianity, it would cause problems for both him and Umeko if it became generally known that he expressed interest in the religion. Itō was very angry when the newspapers wrote that he had advised the emperor to accept Christianity and that all the ministers were in favor of the idea. It was around this time that Umeko began to reconsider her life with the Itōs.

In June, a group of upper class ladies held a charity bazaar at Rokumeikan and Umeko was one of the committee members. She believed it was a way to expand the social horizons of the participants, and wrote Adeline a lively description of how the ladies, who belonged to a class that never talked about money and who had never sold anything in their lives, underwent a subtle change over the course of the day and how the gentlemen were relieved of their pocket money in trying to please the ladies.

June 15, 1884

The day before the fair I went to Rokumeikan, the hall, and Mrs. Ito and Sutematsu and I and other ladies helped to fix it up a bit, and so we spent nearly the whole day there to the neglect of other duties. Everyone who helped in the fair of course, took great interest in her own table and wanted all the prettiest things and decorations on it. . . . The fair opened, and with the music of the band the guests began to come in. The princesses went all around and selected some of the nicest and prettiest things worth some four hundred dollars, and some were chosen for the court. The foreign Legations also bought a great many things.

Until twelve . . . most of the ladies were very demure and quiet, only selling when people chose to buy. But you should have seen the change afterward. I never would have believed it of these quiet ladies, the most of whom think talking of money, of bargaining, or anything of that kind, is a sort of disgrace, and, you know, in Japan these high ladies never attend to money matters or touch a cent of money themselves. Well, they got a good lesson. I suppose they caught it from the few of us who don't mind. Anyhow, after the first, the way they urged the people to buy and praised their own goods, and brought their own particular friends to their own particular table, and actually forced them to buy—if you could have seen the way in which the gentlemen were really robbed of all their money by the persuasion of the ladies, you would not have believed that these were the shy proper dames of Tokio. . . . Nearly everyone went out with big bundles all wrapped up and fixed. When any of us would see anyone we knew, we grew excited fearing he would go to another table and buy, and Mr. Masuda, Shige's brother, was seized on all sides by the ladies, as he is so well known and, poor man, he *had* to buy. The papers are full of the fair and how the ladies came out, and how *dreadfully* skillful they are in showing off goods and in drawing out the yen. At first we found the things priced too cheap, and prices kept going up, instead of coming down, and to make the most of our profits, we often did not give back small change! Many of the gentlemen were very liberal and spent a great deal.

Umeko's mother Hatsuko was expecting another child, but her sister Kotoko had moved out because her husband had returned from abroad.[9] Umeko made this her excuse for leaving the Itō household in mid-June.

Azabu
Sunday
June 23, 1884

. . . Ordinarily our home is very busy, even in everyday life, with the children and the large house, we have plenty to do, but at such a time, and by all laws of Japanese custom, and of ordinary human nature I must come home, and be home, and stay home. . . . I have considered and decided . . . to give up teaching at school and privately during July and August. . . . I am very sorry to give up teaching, but I can't help it, and . . . it would be called heartless if I were not at home during Mother's sickness to help her, and the children and the house. . . . Mrs. Ito bid me go, and said your duty is to your mother and I can't keep you. If your sister is married and not home, then you must help.

In Japan, a girl's duty beyond anything is to parents; when married, the duty passed to the husband's relations, and her own parents no longer expect anything of her. . . . Mr. and Mrs. Ito have said nothing to prevent me, and I do not know if they will ask me to return there

---

9   Umeko's brother-in-law, Ueno Eizaburō (1857–1925), studied mathematics at Dōshisha under Niijima Jō and taught mathematics at Gakunōsha, Tsuda Sen's school. This led to his meeting and marrying Kotoko. He later became a businessman and went to America for some years. He gave both financial and moral support to his sister-in-law Umeko in the management of her school.

again. I hardly think so, because now they do not really need me. The young lady can take her lessons at school in English if need be and she has had a good training now about foreign clothes, and foreign guests are very few. Another reason that Mr. Ito will not ask me to come again, is that all the papers and everywhere are so much against him for his favorable policy to Christianity and scores of enemies are formed on that account. It will be politic in him, as he is not really so favorable to Christianity as they say, if he did not keep in his house a Christian girl . . . I should hate to do him harm in his present position. He may feel relieved if I go.

Of course, you may see, I have some anxiety at this time and in the coming weeks, and it is a mingled feeling with which I leave the Itos'. Kind they have been beyond measure, luxurious the life, and yet I was a stranger, and the formalities and politeness and distantness were often strange to free and easy-going Ume. I feel that it was a very rich experience, an experience most helpful and useful, and insight into a new phase of life, a new lesson from which I shall reap rewards, and I shall never regret the peep into the rank so different from mine, so different from America. I feel too it is a thing all ended. I shall never go back again, I think. . . .

As evident in this letter, Umeko was always thankful for the value of her experiences and she made use of them as steps to the future. In every situation, she made an effort to improve her relationships with other people, remaining sensitive to the workings of the world, but staying true to her mission while respecting other people and their position.

Years later, in 1909, after Itō was assassinated in Harbin, Umeko wrote her personal recollections of the man. The essay was written in English and displays her keen powers of observation as well as the high estimation in which she held Itō.

. . . In later years, when he became Prime Minister he had of cource [sic] to seclude himself, but in those early days,[10] all could reach him who tried. He always listened to anyone, —servant, woman or child who wished to speak to him. He even went out of his way to ask the opinion of inferiors where he thought it would be valuable. He understood human nature as few did, it appealed to him, and human beings were to him of the deepest interest. This more than anything else was his magic wand as a statesman, for he knew how to use his men, and to make them loyal, by giving himself to them unstintingly. . . .

In a conversation of the future life I distinctly remember he said—"I have no religious belief in a future life, but life and death to me are alike. I have no fear of what may come in the future." But though he often spoke of himself as without religion, that he had faith in an unknown power was clearly shown on many occasions.[11]

It seems to me that much of what Umeko says of Itō is applicable to Umeko herself. She believed in him because his aspirations for the time in which they lived were similar to her own.

In the same essay, Umeko recounts a story about Mrs. Itō before her marriage, when the young Itō, who supported the cause of the Meiji Revolution, was pursued by assailants. She hid her lover under the floorboards and a tatami mat and calmly sat upon them until the pursuers gave up and went away.

Umeko wrote to Adeline that "it was a glorious end of a glorious life" and that she had sent her "Personal Recollections of Prince Ito" to Alice Bacon and asked her to have the essay published if possible. The essay is

---

10 When Umeko was a member of his household.
11 *Tsuda Umeko bunsho*, 494–96.

included in a Japanese collection of Umeko's writings, but it is unknown when and where it was published in America, or if it was published at all.

The summer after Itō's death, which occurred after she had established her school, Umeko spent a holiday in Kamakura and took the opportunity to call upon his widow. Mrs. Itō was living a secluded life of retirement, but she was delighted to see Umeko and the two women spent time reminiscing about events long ago.

The youthful Umeko, full of fresh, young vitality, had captured the attention of a formidable politician at the height of his powers, and he spared no effort in supporting her subsequent efforts as an educator. For Umeko, on the other hand, Itō's manly attractions, together with his failings and the cloud of imputations that surrounded him, must have been a dark, disturbing presence in her mind. It was probably her sensitivity to this presence that made it possible for her to empathize with his wife.

CHAPTER
7
WAITING

Soon after Umeko left the Itōs, Shimoda Utako called on her at her family home. It was Utako's first visit and she came in very formal dress, bringing a present.

July 20, 1884

. . . such a polite, refined, gentle lady, and so accomplished. I do admire her and she is one that could well set an example to so many rough, pushing Americans—the contrast grows upon me daily.

The visit apparently had to do with a plan, sponsored by Itō, to join Utako's Tōyō Girl's School to the government-affiliated Peeresses' School. Umeko was to teach at the school and receive a government salary. This would open her way to a future as an educator, and Umeko was happy with the expectation of a stable income and some independence. She was nineteen years old at the time. Umeko would be twenty in December and mused that she would be "turning a full corner" in her life. (She was born on December 31, 1864.)

Umeko had made up her mind to devote her life to education. The words "Oh! that I were more worthy of it, more fitted to be a worker in the vineyard!" in one of her letters[1] stopped me in my tracks. For some reason, they linger in my mind. Umeko was thinking back on more than ten years of study abroad at government expense and no doubt telling herself that she must repay the debt. Her patriotism took the form of a sense of obligation, and it flitted and flickered throughout her life like a will-o'-the-wisp, expressed here and there in different ways, never extinguished

---

1   A letter dated July 29, 1884.

and never forgotten. Sutematsu repeated the same sentiment in her letters to Alice Bacon. Maybe it was the spirit of the times and shared by many. Or maybe it was only a small group around Umeko and Sutematsu who felt that way. No doubt there was a spirit of the times that connected and resonated among people of that era, but Umeko's being a woman would have given her a resolve different from that of men like Itō, who were also deeply invested in the future of their country. It was an era when everything was being transformed; yet women were still expected to submit to men. Umeko dreamt of equal status and individual lives for women. Her every word and action would be open to censure from those around her, which meant that lonely prayer was all she had to fill the spaces of her inner world as she went about her day-to-day life.

July 29, 1884

. . . Pray for me. . . . It is one of the hardest things in the world to be alone in sympathy, or to face the multitude as not one of them—to act unlike the throng, and yet our religion itself makes us just that. . . . The time may come, and we hope it is near, when we shall be the majority, and we shall triumph, and yet that time seems very far off. . . .

It was nearly two years since Umeko came home, and she now had a regular income of sorts and was more or less financially independent. This was also true of Shigeko, who was married but had a teaching position at a music school. And of course there was Shimoda Utako, a paragon of independent womanhood. Still, they were a tiny minority among Japanese women.

Umeko looked around and realized that if a woman wanted a life of her own, the priority was to become financially independent, and yet she knew that few professions were open to women. In order to make them the social equals of men, they had to be educated and they had to be educated as professionals. This being the case, she would devote her life to educating women to become teachers, since teaching was a profession relatively accessible to them, even in that time and age.

Both Shimoda Utako and Ōyama Sutematsu were members of a committee set up to establish the Peeresses' School—Utako because she already had a career as an educator, and Sutematsu because she was the wife of a minister and also Japan's only female college graduate. With these examples before her, Umeko began to think that her own education was not sufficient to realize her dream of improving women's lives by taking a leading role in establishing a new way of educating Japanese women of the future.

That said, for the next stage in her life, she wrote to the principal of the Archer Institute in America to ask for her high school diploma and a testimonial, which were required to qualify as a teacher at the Peeresses' School. The ship carrying the reply to her letter ran out of fuel in the middle of the Pacific Ocean and was forced to make a stop in the Ogasawara Islands. Sailors had to chop wood in the mountains to resupply, and to Umeko's great relief, the ship arrived in Yokohama more than a month late, but carrying the documents she impatiently awaited.

Mrs. Archer, head of the Archer Institute, was apparently a temperamental woman who was apt to take her bad moods out on her students, so Umeko worried until she actually read the testimonial. Contrary to her misgivings, the letter lavished praise on her and ensured her a position at the Peeresses' School.

February 7, 1885

. . . I am glad that she is so sweet and balmy and that her character as a private person is different from the school ma'am. She seems very easy and kind now, and as for the document, I [would] much rather have it as it is now, than as a formal certificate, and the allusion to deportment is very flattering, I am sure.

Interspersed with such reports are inquiries about her pet cat, comments on morning glory seeds she had sent Adeline, talk about her father's cow and its pasturage and milk, criticism of the missionaries, and gossip about dresses and parties.

When Umeko lived with the Lanmans in Georgetown, she had a cat named "Necko" ["cat" in Japanese], which reminds me of a dog in my old American neighborhood that was named "Inu" ["dog" in Japanese]. "Does Necko still exist, and do you pet her any? I have no time nowadays for pets; my pets to scold and fondle are the children, and they are enough, I can tell you."[2] Umeko always referred to her students and younger sisters as "children" and seemed truly fond of youngsters. Caring for them and teaching them were apparently in no way burdensome to her.

Around this time, Itō reformed the nobility by modeling it on European peerage systems. Umeko's comments on this are somewhat ambivalent.

October 7, 1884

Did I tell you that the government has settled that the nobility must have a decided dress, that is, for state occasions? The ladies have, for full dress, something resembling that worn at court of most gorgeous brocades and with much purple and red, so different from the ordinary street dress and dress worn now. The court dress is really beautiful, and it will make the dressing at all the great balls and state occasions very gorgeous and gay. The movement is not bad, for why is the foolish custom now prevailing to wear such simple stuff

---

2   From the letter dated July 29, 1884.

with no embroidery, when such rich stuffs are in plenty here? Now foreign dress too is allowed and that is very gay too. Sutematsu and many of those foreignized ladies will wear foreign dresses, for that is a great fashion now. The hair of these ladies is very different from the complicated fixings now. It is left hanging simply down the back and tied, but in the front, the hair is puffed all around in a way quite indescribable. Mrs. Ito and all those people will have to do that way soon. The rule does not take place until New Year's, and the papers say that all the looms in Kioto are as busy as can be, fulfilling orders, for nothing can be gotten that is not ordered first, and that some time beforehand.

I am sorry that your morning-glories turned out so badly, but in Japan one can never tell exactly what species will be the variegated, and which will be the usual species. It is said, however, that it is not a yearly thing by any means and if it is not variegated and curious-shaped this year, it may be next, so take these seeds and plant them again. Usually only one seed in seven has the peculiarity and all the rest are the usual, but if these latter seeds are planted and its seeds taken, the peculiarity, or deformity, again appears in after plants. . . .

I did not tell you that, since the other day, we have had a cow on the place. Father concluded to try keeping one, and as we have lots of room, and pasturage, and lots of children to enjoy milk, I think it is a good idea. The whole family are taking to milk drinking, and will grow fat on it, I suppose. I wish that I liked it, and could drink it now that we have such a nice cow, and fresh milk in plenty, but I can not take a bit. I do not think Mother nor Aunt really likes it, but they take it as medicine. I can not take it for that even, but then I can make lots of custards and nice things with plenty of milk, so it is very nice to have it. The children are fond of it, and I suppose we will soon have fat, rosy, country cheeks. The cow seems to give plenty of milk and sometimes we have a great oversupply. I think if we could have a sort of dairy out here, it would be very nice.

July 14, 1884

. . . He [Mr. Ito] is in favor of an aristocracy, and . . . [is working in] preparation for the national assembly to be held in seven years from now, the nobles probably forming some sort of a body like the House of Lords, though it can not be said that there is an over amount of brains in this class. They are an idle class, it is acknowledged on the whole. Of course, everyone has been much interested in all this turn of affairs, and the papers have been full of it. The ministers, or *sangi*, have all been raised to the rank of the *daimios* . . . the corresponding title in English being Count, I think. . . . Therefore, Sutematsu becomes by this a countess. Countess Oyama she is to be called. A very empty title, as she herself said, and most absurd, but nevertheless hers in right, and that is what she is to be called in truth. . . . It all sounds very fine, it seems to me, in name at least, and it may have some effect on the Europeans, at any rate.

Umeko ended her long letter of July 29, 1884, with the following words:

I have spun and spun this thread of words and letters with my pen, until I have finished my structure of the letter, and now my head is as empty as a silkworm's is, after it is done, and I think I too must go to sleep. It is too lovely a night with the glorious moon to sleep, but I am tired with the day's regular work and I must rest.

1885 dawned, and in September, Umeko joined the teaching staff of the Peeresses' School on the recommendation of Itō Hirobumi. Shimoda

Utako was director of the school, and in this way, the girls' division of Gakushūin [which originated in Kyoto as a school for the nobility] became an independent institution under the jurisdiction of the ministry of the imperial household.

In December, a cabinet system came into existence; Itō Hirobumi became the first prime minister of Japan and Mori Arinori was appointed minister of education. During the New Year's holiday of 1886, Umeko called on Itō's wife and daughters and came to realize the impact of Itō's rise to Japan's highest position of power.

January 7, 1886

. . . The government has been entirely changed, officials have been cut down one-third, and salaries reduced and, in fact, everything topsy-turvy. Whether it will be for better or for worse, I don't know, and, of course, politicians are excited. I don't care very much one way or another, except for the good of Japan.

What was happening between Japan and the rest of the world at this time? Rokumeikan, the iconic guest palace launched in November 1883 was hosting numerous Western-style balls where high government officials entertained foreign ambassadors and legations, and Japanese women feverishly imitated Western fashions with the help of people like Umeko, who advised Itō's daughters on how to dress.

July 1, 1886

We hear that foreign dress is to be introduced at court, and the Empress is ordering her wardrobe from Europe, and it will come soon. . . . The present court dress is not all that is convenient and comfortable, but it is pretty and dignified and they are used to it, but they are going to make themselves a laughing stock by too much imitation of the foreigners. Think of low neck and squeezed waists being enforced in Japan, and I hear they are going to adopt the rules of the court of England, and that, you know, requires low neck and short sleeves on every occasion. . . . They are throwing away the good of their native land together with the evil. The Empress will also begin one of the foreign languages—I don't know which. I don't envy whoever teaches her—it will be so much trouble and bother, and one would be afraid to move. All this is Mr. Ito's doing. I think he is going too far—should like to tell him so, but don't have any chance to do so at all.

Fancy dress balls were held at Rokumeikan and also at the prime minister's residence in Nagata-chō. Umeko considered dressing up as a historical figure—probably Ushiwakamaru.[3] She also debated the possibility of borrowing an old dress from an aunt, who may have been Takeko—the aunt who waited on the Tokugawa family—or perhaps another relative. Fancy dress or otherwise, Umeko was like Bigot in considering traditional Japanese costumes to be more gorgeous and beautiful than Western dresses. But that is how foreign eyes would see Japan, whereas Japanese might take exception to having so-called Japanese things continually imposed on them by outsiders.

September 18, 1886

. . . The invitations for the ball on the Emperor's birthday are out, but I declare I am not going. Stematz will not go, and Shige can't, and I do

---

3   Ushiwakamaru was the childhood name of Minamoto no Yoshitsune (1159–1189), a military commander of the Minamoto clan in the late Heian period. He is a legendary hero who supposedly showed great prowess as a fighter from early boyhood.

not want to. It is a jam and a crush, and not a bit of pleasure—pretty to see but tiresome year after year in succession—don't you think so. You see I am getting so old I feel that I am losing the novelty of ball, and yet not gaining a fondness for it at all.

The empress often visited the Peeresses' School to observe lessons and Umeko fretted because her students did not read well. She wrote with some humor[4] that no one would understand what they were saying anyway, so they should just read along. She also reported that the empress dowager invited all the students of the school to a circus performance and that they went in jinrikshas—all two hundred of them.

Umeko had more or less given up on marriage, but some time ago, there had been rumors of an engagement between herself and Kanda Naibu. Kanda, who was a baron, had studied in the United States and played Bassanio in a performance of the *Merchant of Venice* with Sutematsu shortly after Umeko and her friends returned from their long years of study. He became a scholar of English and eventually taught at Tokyo Imperial University, Tokyo University of Foreign Languages, Tokyo University of Commerce, Gakushūin, and other institutions.

He apparently proposed marriage to Sutematsu before she married Ōyama, and Sutematsu mentioned in a letter to Alice Bacon a young man she had some feelings for. But Sutematsu decided to marry Ōyama and seems to have played matchmaker for Umeko and Kanda. Kanda fell in with the idea, but Umeko chose work over marriage and Kanda soon married someone else. It is impossible to say if he is the man spoken of in the letter below, but her words give us an idea of Umeko's feelings about marriage. She was twenty years old at the time.

---

4   In a letter dated November 10, 1885.

January 2, 1885

I was much amused by the rumors of my engagement. I don't know how many times people have rumored my engagement out here in Japan. I suppose the reason is that everyone thinks it is high time, and I am hanging out too long and will soon be passé. I let them think so, and go on. I don't think you need hope I might smile on any young man. I don't see any young man to smile on, of any kind or sort or variety, and when I do occasionally meet one, I have to be very formal in the Japanese way. I am too satisfied as I am, and I fear I could not get along well in any matrimonial yoke. . . . I want no made marriage, with any unknown, and no money nor rank nor position could tempt me. Do make up your mind to see me an old maid. No one can say for a certainty anything but I think any marriage is very far off for me, nay, almost an impossibility. And I am real passé now. Maybe I could not find anyone if I began the search, unless some old widower—there aren't any young men left—sad fact!! I don't know how old maids get along out in Japan, but one must try it, and see how it is anyhow.

Umeko writes with wit and humor; her words are straightforward but rich in undertones and paradox. She was by no means afraid of men and did not dislike them. In fact, she was normally attracted to the opposite sex and being a young woman overflowing with vitality, I am certain that men found her attractive.

That she was neither brusque nor dry, that she was not a masculine, no-nonsense, action-only type of woman, is clear from her letters, which reveal a surprising range of topics, a natural expressiveness, and great emotional sensitivity. She may have been impetuous and somewhat short-tempered, but she was flexible and soon became reasonable again, and more than anything else, she was sensitive to the feelings of others. That is, she had imagination, and she had a way with language. I really cannot understand why the men of the Meiji era left her alone. It is possible that many looked on her favorably from a distance but were afraid to approach, or that Umeko maintained a stubbornly impassable façade. That must have been it, I think.

March 16, 1887

You know that there has been a great deal of talk in Japan, in the paper and everywhere, about women—women's sphere, women's education, and the position of women in Japan, dress, manners, etc. There has been also in the newspapers a great deal about these women of doubtful reputation—the singing and dancing girls who appear at so many entertainments. . . . Sutematsu and I talked the matter over, and thought it was a perfect shame that these women did all the entertaining, leaving nothing to the ladies to do in reality, and by their appearing in society and mingling with the men, they become first the mistresses and finally the true wives of the finest and highest-ranked gentlemen. Such was the case with Mrs. Ito, Mrs. Kuki, Mrs. Yoshida, and dozens of others, while the young girls are left in the cold. There is this to say in excuse: that the young ladies have been until now most stupid and least to be desired as wives and so it was natural that men chose the bright *geishas*. But now everything is different, and so this custom ought to be changed. . . .

In other words, Japanese men stayed away from non-professional women, and this made it impossible for ordinary women to meet men in a legitimate manner. There was no way for them to find husbands on their own. Society was very hard on women who tried to live modern, Westernized lives, and

Umeko shook her head disbelievingly at the numerous scandalous rumors being spread about the wife of Mori Arinori, Sutematsu, and Utako.

February 22, 1887

. . . I told you before that she [Mrs. Mori] had become crazy and all that. I do not know whether it is on that account or other reasons which rumor says there are, but anyhow it is certain that she has been *divorced*. Mrs. Mori, after becoming crazy, was placed in another house quite a distance from her present dwelling, and there she lived for nearly a year, and now just lately she has been divorced. Of course, this has caused great talk, [for] Mr. Mori, of all persons, to go and do such a thing. You know he was the first man that ever had a foreign wedding ceremony, and he had witnesses and swore never to part from her . . . so I don't see how he can . . . divorce her until he has a better reason than that she is crazy. And rumor is . . . that she has not been constant to her husband, and that this mere fact has made her crazy, or that his finding it out made her so, etc., and as the whole thing is a mystery, of course people talk about it all the more. Whichever side is wrong . . . everyone blames the woman as a matter of course. . . . Is it not a dreadful thing? And a year or so ago no one was more envied than Mrs. Mori, as Mr. Mori certainly seemed good to her, and he never runs after these singing girls [as] so many men do, and Mrs. Mori was such a homely person with no pretensions to beauty, and having been married for love, from a very ordinary family, it was no wonder people said that she was a lucky person. And so the change is more sudden for that. But I can not see that a person of that rank, with her husband always with her, and with her three children and all—I don't see how a woman could have gone astray, especially such a *quiet, gentle*, submissive body as she seemed, and so kind and good, too. I have always admired her. If Mr. Mori has gotten tired of her only, and lets these idle stories go around about her, then he is a worse man than I ever thought. But if these stories are true, then he is much to be pitied indeed. . . . But no one can tell what is what, and the mystery about it makes it all the worse.

The gossip about Mrs. Mori, Tsune, was that she had had an affair in London that resulted in a child born after the family's return to Japan. Her lover was an Englishman attached to the Japanese legation, or, in another version, a foreigner she met at a Rokumeikan ball. And contrary to Umeko's impression, Tsune is said to have been a flamboyant woman. In any case, Mori was remarried to the fifth daughter of the influential statesman Iwakura Tomomi soon afterward. It was Itō who proposed the match. Umeko's sympathies leaned toward the divorced first wife, however, and it displeased her that people rushed to blame the woman when nobody really knew the facts of the matter.

It also irked Umeko that her family was disappointed when her sister Kotoko gave birth to a daughter, and that the birth or death of a princess was given such short shrift in the imperial family. Aside from the Mori scandal, the general situation regarding adultery was that men often kept other women and sometimes had their wives bring up the resulting offspring. Women, on the other hand, were subject to laws forbidding extramarital intercourse, and if a woman went so far as to have an illicit child, the uproar was such that she could easily be hounded into insanity. Part of the attack on the Moris was motivated by a general unhappiness with the Westernizing policies of the new government, but what mattered to Umeko was the situation of the women.

November 28, 1887

. . . Mrs. Shimoda is now sick and in bed. . . . I think her sickness is more than half on account of all this talk about her, although she is very delicate anyhow and has bronchitis. I am sorry for the poor woman, but she has a great many enemies, of course, on account of her prominent position, as being the head of such a large school, as this is. I wonder when they will cease scandal and gossip all over the world. I am glad that all that talk about Sutematsu has nearly ceased, but she does not go out so much nowadays as she used to do. General Ōyama is away yet, in the country, and she is all alone with the children.

Charles Lanman had written to Umeko that he wanted to publish a book about her, and Umeko replied in another part of the letter above that although she may have had an interesting and promising childhood, she had not really done anything yet. She thought a book about her would be premature, but promised to consider the matter carefully. However, in the next mail, she answered in the following way:

December 7, 1887

. . . The more I have thought about Mr. Lanman's letter, the more I am inclined to think that to wait a little would be the wisest course. . . . You see, Japan is in such a whirl now, and the question of women's education etc. being so much agitated that any woman as Mrs. Shimoda or Sutematsu, who is in any way prominent or well known, is picked to pieces by the old school people, who are against the new code, and you see the dreadful stories they get up against them.[5] Of course,

---

5   One such scandal asserted that Sutematsu had an affair with a groom.

there are political reasons, too. . . . I am always glad I did not stay at the Itos', on that account, and came home before Mr. Ito became Prime Minister, and before the question of women's place, rank, etc. was brought up so much. As it is, I am only too delighted to go on my own quiet way, not having anyone's jealousy or envy to say bad things of me. Japan has not quite made up its mind yet, whether women may have the same freedom as men. She is trying to find flaws in all who have gone ahead of time. I would rather for one year anyhow not be brought into too much notice. All this fuss has not lasted a year yet, and will blow over in as much time again. I give you frankly, without the least concealment, all the reasons for not publishing now, and now will leave it to you entirely. . . . Mr. Lanman will understand, I am sure, and will use his judgement, and I will leave it to him. . . .

Umeko worried about this and that, became angry at certain things, and worked furiously at everything; meanwhile, Japan and the world also moved forward.

1881 Meiji Life Insurance Company is founded. Tokyo Gas Company and Nippon Yūsen (Japan Mail Shipping Line) are established in 1885.

1882 The Imperial Rescript to Soldiers and Sailors is issued. Tokyo College (precursor of Waseda University) is established in this year, followed by Tokyo School of Commerce (precursor of Hitotsubashi University) in 1884 and Tokyo School of Music (precursor of Tokyo University of the Arts) in 1887.

1882 The Imo Incident, a violent uprising, occurs in Seoul, Korea, and the Japanese legation is attacked.

1884 The Chichibu Incident, a large-scale peasant revolt, takes place in Saitama prefecture, immediately west of Tokyo.

1885 *Jogaku zasshi* (Journal of Women's Studies), Japan's first magazine for women is launched. Jiji News Agency is established, and *Tokyo Asahi Shimbun* and *Osaka Mainichi Shimbun* are first issued in 1888.

1885 Tsubouchi Shōyō's *Tōsei shosei katagi* (The Character of Modern Students) and *Shōsetsu shinzui* (The Essence of the Novel) are published. Futabatei Shimei's *Ukigumo* (Floating Clouds) follows in 1887.

1886 Burma is annexed by British India.

1886 The American Federation of Labor (AFL) is founded in the U.S.

1886 Carl Benz applies for a patent for the world's first motor car.

1887 Indochina is consolidated under French rule.

1887 Regulations for Japanese private railways are set forth and Nippon Beer Company comes into existence. Kanegafuchi Spinning Company (Kanebo) is founded in 1888.

This was the state of the world as Itō launched his program of political reformation.

January 20, 1886

. . . Great changes are taking place in the government. Mr. Ito is doing them, and great discontent exists. But the government is making a bold plunge for the better and outsiders consider it a grand change. Mr. Ito, I hear, rarely leaves his office or his home for fear of assassination from some of those turned out of office. I suppose a thousand or two office holders are turned out, and their work to be done by the remaining, thus cutting down all expenses and making the number of officers fewer. The Foreign Department, the Educational Bureau, and others have made the changes. The Department of the Royal

Household, under which I am and of which Mr. Ito is head, has not yet made any changes, but they are daily expected. As the number of higher rank officers has been limited, and everything cut down, though I know I will not be discharged, I may have my salary cut down or my rank as *so nin* altered. . . . Of course, I do not know, but I am waiting. . . .

Umeko worried, but her position remained stable. In November 1886 she became a professor, she was given a slight promotion in rank, and her annual salary was raised to five hundred yen. Shimoda Utako and Umeko were the only women to be given the rank of *sōninkan* (senior officials), and Utako, as head of the school, received an annual salary of 1,500 yen or more. "Perhaps Mr. Ito begins to realize that foreign dress is very expensive as his wife and daughters have adopted it, and that for foreign tastes the 35 yen a month is too little, and so my salary was raised," she wrote with some humor in her letter of November 23.

After becoming a teacher at the Peeresses' School, Umeko frequently came into contact with people of the upper classes. The empress often visited the school, and at New Year's, she presented each of the teachers with a length of silk.

> . . . We had to enter before her and receive it from one of the gentlemen officials. . . . Everyone . . . think[s] so much of a present from the Empress. It is very fine indeed. I think I must have a Japanese dress [made] of it, as it is not good for foreign dress, and there is not enough of it.[6]

---

6   From a letter dated February 11, 1886.

The crown prince also visited the school.

> . . . He is still a wee bit of a fellow, being only ten years old. I wonder what he thought of so many rows and rows of girls as there were. The poor little fellow seemed quite bewildered, and I don't suppose it interested him very much.[7]

Umeko introduced tennis to the school and wrote that she wanted the children to learn as many outdoor games as possible. She herself seems to have enjoyed sports as a girl and Adeline frequently suggested that she was putting on weight because she was not getting enough exercise.

When I was a student at Tsuda College, the school placed great importance on physical exercise and we had lessons in tennis, hockey, and girls' baseball. This was no doubt a reflection of the founder's conviction that education should nurture both mind and body.

On the other hand, Umeko was not particularly enthusiastic about dancing at this time.

March 7, 1887

> . . . [He] sends me an invitation to a dance on the steamer for next Thursday, but, of course, I can not accept. In the first place, I have no chaperone and in the second, I can't get off from school in the afternoon, and then I haven't a dress, and then I do not know whether I want to go or not. On the whole I think I would like to go to see what it is like, so that I might go were it not for the other objections. It is very kind of him to send the invitation though I can't accept it.

---

7   From a letter dated October 9, 1886.

March 16, 1887

I called on the Itos the other day and found them all at home, and pleasant as ever. Mr. Ito said that he was planning to have a fancy ball, the first one in Japan. I suppose, as he told me about it, I will be expected to go and will receive an invitation, though I am sure I would gladly do without one. It will be such a bother and nuisance for me to think up a costume and I think I will refuse. People who have nothing to do can afford to spend their time getting up costumes and think about their dresses, but I have neither the time nor the money for it. What will happen next in Japan now that they have gotten to fancy balls and all that?

Balls and Western fashions were all the rage, which seemed silly to Umeko, and she thought the Japanese were making a laughing stock of themselves. She commented that it would no doubt continue until the foreigners got used to them and stopped laughing.

Sutematsu was to make an appearance in court at New Year's and she was obliged to have a dress made up with a low neck and short sleeves in the English fashion, which she was unhappy about. She was often sick for various reasons and Umeko worried that she was as thin as a rail. Sutematsu had given birth to a son in February 1886 and her husband Iwao was overjoyed to have a son after four daughters. When Umeko went to congratulate them, he pretended to be disappointed and made a joke of it.

> . . . he was very merry joking about the baby, and making out to be very sorry and disappointed that it was not a girl, but adding in fun that it would have been a dreadful thing if it had been a girl, for it is such an ugly baby, but as it is a boy it will not make any difference. . . .[8]

8   From a letter dated February 19, 1886.

In addition to teaching children of the imperial family and other nobility at the Peeresses' School, Umeko was also asked to tutor some of the children individually. One of these was a daughter of the Kujō family—a seven-and-a-half year old girl named Nori—and it came about that Umeko should teach her over the summer holiday. Umeko had planned to go to Nikkō with foreign friends, so the girl was sent along in the company of a maid. The Kujōs gave Umeko a hundred yen to settle accounts for their daughter and the servant during the three weeks and left all the arrangements to her. Her friends Mr. and Mrs. Page spoke no Japanese and the hotel staff and the girl's maid spoke no English, so everything fell on Umeko's shoulders.

In Nikkō, she and the girl slept in a hotel near the Pages that catered exclusively to upper-class clientele, but Umeko took her meals with her friends, and had the girl come to her for lessons every day and took her for walks. They made an excursion into the surrounding mountains, with Umeko on horseback and the child and her maid in a sedan chair.

Umeko remembered that she herself had been sent to America more than a decade before at the age of seven, and commented on the way the Kujōs sent their young daughter away so casually:

> . . . I am more and more surprised that the parents of the girl let her come, as it is the first time that she has ever left home, and to come with me, a perfect stranger, and to go to foreigners is a wonder. . . . I feel the responsibility and would like to feel perfectly free, yet I am very glad to be able to do what I can for her, and can't help it if she finds it dull or lonely. I try to let her have a good time and she seems to be picking up English very nicely. She is such a dear, sweet thing— not a bit shy as so many children are, and she makes friends with all she has anything to do with.[9]

---

9   From a letter dated August 17, 1886.

When Umeko dealt with young girls, her comments glowed with the joy of watching their lives unfold, and she often wrote in her letters how much she liked to teach people and see them grow. Around this time, Umeko began to express a desire to study abroad once more, and she also joined a society that discussed women's education and women's problems in general.[10]

Many members of the group had studied at the Normal School, which trained teachers, and they met once a month for lectures. Sometimes one or two of the women spoke briefly about women's problems, and Umeko took her turn and talked about health care and nursing. She stills seems to have had difficulty in speaking correct Japanese, for she wrote the lecture in English, had it translated into Japanese, and read it out. She commented in a letter that it should be Sutematsu doing things like this and expressed disappointment that Sutematsu had given herself up to being only Mrs. Ōyama.

Umeko's recent contact with women of the upper classes had made her more dubious than ever about the position of women in Japan. She occasionally observed that Japan's upper classes had no morality at all and that the middle and lower classes were at least somewhat better. She read the English translation of a novel written by a woman (probably the *Tale of Genji*) and commented that it was a good book for understanding Japan, but so full of immorality that young girls could not possibly be permitted to read it, and that it would never find a place in an American library. But it was poetic and evoked a strange, dreamlike world, she added. In any event, she was deeply interested in Japanese literature as a way to understand Japan.

Being in daily contact with daughters of the upper classes, Umeko was in a position to witness the substance and mechanisms of authority in the Japanese state, and in that sense, must have arrived at a sensibility similar to that of Murasaki Shikibu, the brilliant lady-in-waiting of the Heian imperial court who wrote the *Tale of Genji*.

---

10 The group is mentioned in a letter dated May 6, 1886.

Born in the late nineteenth century and sent abroad at a young age to be educated according to the needs of national policy, Umeko experienced life in two worlds separated by an ocean and became adept in two languages, which gave great scope to her powers of observation.

January 14, 1887

> ... when I do [go to court], I shall have to have some sort of a dress, and it will cost a fortune, so I would rather not go, but will content myself with being presented to the Empress on less formal occasions as when she visits school. A full court dress will be required hereafter at court on state occasions, and this will scare most ladies away. I think they are all very foolish to make so much of dress. Why don't they try and improve schools or society instead of dress. . . .

When people live with a strange language, primitive instincts awaken. If you don't understand the language, you are not deceived by words. You become aware of the way the foreign language imposes its persuasions on you, which you may find impressive or occasionally appalling, but at the same time, you also become aware of the contrivances and deceit of your mother tongue, which you formerly accepted with no thought at all.

Umeko had been home for three years and was getting more and more comfortable with Japanese in day-to-day situations, but she was still more fluent in English. She stood between two languages, but her identity lay with the country of Japan and its people, and especially with the women who comprised half of that people, and she was convinced that her bond with them was the one she must live by. State-run schools followed national policy, and she found it irksome that the policy was not necessarily in line with her own visions.

Thus Umeko began to nurture an earnest desire to establish a school of her own—a private school. She wanted to be more than just an English teacher, but in order to head a private school, she would need an education comparable at least to Sutematsu's college degree. Sutematsu was older than Umeko and had been in America for the same number of years, and she had come home with a degree from Vassar Women's College. In the beginning, Umeko hoped to contribute to Japanese women's education by assisting Sutematsu, but now that Sutematsu was married and wrapped up in her family, it was up to Umeko. In which case, she would need to be more highly educated.

Umeko had already studied for more than ten years at national expense, so she could not ask the government to bear the full cost again. However, if the Peeresses' School where she taught would continue to pay her salary and permit her to study in America for two or three years, it might be possible to realize her plan.

There was mention of Charles Lanman selling some of the essays she had written in Japan to American publishers, so she may have considered that as a possible supplement to her income. She also wrote to Adeline to ask how much it would cost to study at a first-rate institution.

Her present education might suffice for an ordinary teacher, but Umeko had higher aspirations. She wanted to educate women in order to liberate them as human beings. With this great vision in her heart, Umeko unwaveringly went about her daily work as a teacher and even enjoyed it. The most pleasant aspect of Umeko's letters is the way she found joy in the vitality of her young charges. Many aspects of the Peeresses' School must have struck Umeko as stiff and comical, but she observed people in an amazingly straightforward way and had an excellent grasp of reality and its situations.

Observing people from stations of life different from her own, she judged them fairly and was never obsequious or sycophantic, but neither was she discourteous to people of rank in situations that required that they be treated in a specific way. She recognized the differences between the imperial household, the nobility, the peerage, the various classes, and people of all personalities, and saw them for what they were: manifestations of the way human beings construct a society.

When the empress ordered a dress from Europe that cost twenty thousand dollars, Umeko lamented that the people remained poor and uneducated and complained that it was silly for the Japanese to aspire to Western fashions that didn't suit them. But she heaved a sigh of relief when the empress looked well in her dress, and noted that it was an insult for the musical *Mikado* to make Japan the subject of comic satire for the amusement of Westerners.

> . . . Just suppose, if on the Japanese stage in one of the Tokyo theatres Queen Victoria and the British royal family were made the subject of a ridiculous play, why, the British representative would soon appeal for redress and make a great fuss. But Japan, being the weaker side, can't make a fuss. . . . Can't you send me the libretto of it just for fun? The costumes and all are very, very, absurd, I hear from Japanese, and I should like to see and read it anyhow to judge of it. . . .[11]

Umeko was looking squarely at the fact that foreigners were laughing at the Japanese government and amusing themselves at a musical in which officials and the emperor made fools of themselves.

In September 1886, Umeko responded to a letter from Adeline, who was worried about her safety during a cholera epidemic in Tokyo.

---

11 From a letter probably written on September 23, 1886.

September 20, 1886

. . . I think you hardly recognize the fact that the cholera rarely affects the better classes especially away from the crowded districts of Tokio. I think for instance among the two hundred scholars at school, very few or any lost any of their friends this summer, so it was the exception when any but the poorer ones got the epidemic rather than otherwise.

In this particular year, two or three hundred people were infected daily at one point. One percent of Tokyo's population died of the disease, but the upper classes suffered fewer than a hundred deaths altogether. Jinricksha drivers and laborers bore the worst of the epidemic.

Umeko wrote that she had bought a jinricksha for thirteen dollars. She had been renting one up till then for a dollar and half per month, and paid a man to pull it besides, but so many government officials had lost their jobs because of Itō's reforms that the market was flooded with jinrickshas and they were quite inexpensive. In those days, you could either hire a jinricksha driver with his own vehicle, or you could rent a jinricksha and then hire someone to pull it.

The school was short-staffed and everyone was too busy, Umeko complained, and wrote that they had requested more teachers to no avail.

. . . I think Mr. Ito ought to see that this school at least does not overwork its teachers. The government is spending so much money on buildings, foreign dress, and extravagances of all kinds, while all the officers of the upper classes have a good time and the rest of the people are having a most hard one. But I suppose all this is the fault of every administration in almost every country.[12]

Umeko reacted normally to things and events and was sometimes angry or complaining, but never overly aggressive. When she was aroused and had to fight, she accepted the challenge with pleasure and had a way of looking on the bright side of things. This was probably an inborn temperament, but her Tsuda breeding was no doubt reinforced by the Lanmans' loving cultivation of her natural gifts. The voluminous letters that she continued to write for three decades, expressing her innermost feelings, were like a steady fire stoked by the love that Charles and Adeline Lanman showered upon her.

It seems to me that Umeko's devotion to Christianity was also deeply related to her trust in the Lanmans. The large circle of friends and acquaintances she drew to herself in Japan was also a product of the trust she had learned to place in the positive aspects of human nature.

Umeko's curiosity was scientific in that it linked things in an integrated manner, and in that it was analytic and flexible. For example, her comments on specific subjects such as missionaries, Itō Hirobumi, Japanese culture, and institutions are never one-dimensional. Even when she was critical, she was also loving, and more sensitive to people's merits and virtues than to their faults. Otherwise, how could she have written so harshly of missionaries and yet have missionary friends and continue to live as a Christian? How could she have been so passionate about drawing Japanese women up to her own level?

Memories of her years in America made her sentimental, and she sometimes became lyrical:

---

12 Ibid.

March 4, 1886

. . . How I wish I could sit around with you by the old Franklin stove
this dreary evening and warm myself, and talk to you, and watch the
bright sparks and flames! Oh! America and you all seem very, very far
away, and a great ocean between. Don't you wish we could have a chat
sometimes, and enjoy each other's talk instead of only writing letters
all the time? The days of my childhood seem so far behind, and other
things are crowding them out, and all the American associations and
life and good times all seem so faint and far away. Sometimes it is
hard to realize that I am the same person, so different is it now from
then. I often build air-castles, and think how much I should enjoy
returning to you, and seeing all the old places once again. Do you
think you can't come out to me possibly? If so, then I must go to you
someway, and I will if I can—only be very patient.

Adeline awaited her letters eagerly and fussed when she did not hear from
Umeko regularly. She would press her with repetitions of "I am so anxious"
and "I am so afraid," which exasperated Umeko and made her respond
that there was nothing to worry about, that she was enjoying herself, that
she had nothing to write about that day, or occasionally with a peevish
"Good night! I'm tired and going to bed!" Then she would apologize for
her crabbiness and write another long and detailed letter.

CHAPTER
8
CONNECTIONS

It is the time of year when the mornings and evenings are suddenly cold, although the daytime sun is hot and the tree leaves are changing color day by day. This is the season that always takes me back to the wooded campus where I spent four years of my youth.

Two years ago, during the same season, I visited Bryn Mawr College, a women's college near Philadelphia in the American east. Unlike the Musashino woods of the western Kantō plain, where autumn falls like a shower of golden light, the woods of continental America were a multi-colored tapestry of yellow, orange, red, vermillion, crimson, and browns. Nevertheless, I felt that I had been in that place before.

When I was going to college, we were always being told about the famous women's college in the American east. Tsuda Umeko, founder of our college, had studied there and established a scholarship fund that permitted some of our graduates to go there to study. The ones who came home and took up teaching positions at our college told students about the campus in

Ōba Minako and classmates at Tsuda College in 1949. Ōba is the one reclining on the lawn.

the faraway land. We never saw it, but we felt as if we had, and sometimes we even felt as if we had studied there.

We were like children listening to stories from the Japanese classics. People who grew up in eastern Japan or Kyushu or Hokkaido or Shikoku and never set eyes on the old capitals of Kyoto or Nara or Asuka can hear place names like Hiei, Higashiyama, or Sagano, or mountain names like Mikasayama, Kaguyama, or Futakamiyama, and see them in their minds' eye. Our relationship to Bryn Mawr was something like that.

When Japanese who have read and loved the classics walk for the first time in the foothills of the three famed mountains of Yamato[1] or Mount Miwa, they have the illusion of having come home. Strangely enough, I had the same experience when I visited Bryn Mawr for the first time, a reflection of how often students at Tsuda College were told about Bryn Mawr during their four years at college. In fact, the atmosphere at Tsuda was somewhat similar to Bryn Mawr, or so I thought when I visited Bryn Mawr more than three decades after I graduated from college.

I took a local train from Philadelphia and got off at a small station named Bryn Mawr, which already felt like part of the campus. The ambience of the students passing by, the way someone who looked like faculty answered me when I asked for directions—all of it took me back to my college days, thirty years earlier.

Oddly, my mind also slipped back to a trip I had made to Gyeongju, South Korea, a few years back. There, I felt as if I had been drawn into an old folk tale. I could imagine an old bamboo cutter ambling out from behind the gently rolling hills and nine maidens skipping along with songs

---

1 Kaguyama, Unebiyama, and Miminashiyama are located in present-day Nara prefecture and have been celebrated for their beauty since the late seventh century, when the ancient capital of Fujiwara was built on a plain surrounded by the three peaks.

on their lips.[2] And now, in America, a landscape I had imagined in my mind as a young woman actually unfolded before my eyes, aided by the smile of a stranger.

One stop before the small station of Bryn Mawr is Haverford, the location of the college where Arishima Takeo studied. This led me to recall that Arishima Takeo had committed double suicide with Hatano Akiko, who had a link to Tsuda College. Strange shadowy connections pop up here and there, all over the world. In the U.S. and Canada there are many towns and cities with names like London, Paris, Berlin, Moscow, and Petersburg, and Canada's London even has a river called the Thames. The towns may seem utterly different from the London, Paris, Berlin, and Moscow in England, France, Germany, and Russia. But try standing awhile in one of these places, like an animal in the forest, with your mind's eye open and your ears alert. Observe the shapes of the house windows, the slope of the roofs, the names on the doorplates, the ways the gardens are laid out and flowers are planted. Feel how fragments of the woods, forests, and lakes expand and overlap with fragments of old towns in a homeland regretfully left behind. The New World was built on dreams dreamt in the towns and cities of the old country. Or, as the case may be, students go from the new land to an old capital and bring back to the New World the products of their study. The outcome is a new rendition of an old song.

There are no doubt similar stories about identical place names in different parts of Japan. There are many mountains and temples with Chinese names, and if you follow the paths of the Buddhist monks who founded them and go to China to see the old temples where they studied, you sense a mysterious aura that floats across the barriers of time and space.

---

2   This refers to a scene from an old tale out of the *Manyōshū*, a collection of poetry and prose compiled in the late eighth century. An old bamboo cutter encounters nine young maidens who make sport of him, but he responds by reciting a poem that captivates them.

I have strayed from Umeko's story, but place names aside, there are modes of culture that encounter and connect with other modes in subtle ways, develop their various characteristics in unexpected directions, and become distinctive forms unique to a specific climate.

Just as the golden light that spilled across the leafy branches of the Musashino woods was different from the continental autumn colors that dyed the woods of Bryn Mawr, the golden-haired and brown-haired girls at Bryn Mawr spoke a different language from the girls in Japan. But behind the words was something that came from even farther away. I am told that the colonists who settled Bryn Mawr originally came from somewhere in Wales.

Let us go back one hundred years to the story of Tsuda Umeko.

Umeko left Japan in July 1889 to study once again in America at Bryn Mawr College. The idea of another course of study abroad seems to have been simmering in her mind from the time she began to teach at the Peeresses' School. Standing at a lectern, she had begun thinking about women's education from the vantage point of a young woman of the new age. The Peeresses' School was controlled by policymakers who followed the ideology of officialdom, which was an ideology of state and education that placed men at the center of everything. Needless to say, Meiji Japan had great dreams for the new nation, and Meiji men had sent young girls like Umeko, Sutematsu, and Shigeko abroad for more than ten years of study precisely because they also had dreams of a new type of woman. They hoped that these women would bring something home from the distant land beyond the sea to scatter new seeds in Japan.

The women, on the other hand, came home after ten and more years of study to find members of their own sex downtrodden and beleaguered in the shadows of the men who administered the rapidly developing new nation. The so-called "new women" of the day were of the upper classes and comical imitators of Western manners. Umeko's descriptions of these shallow-minded compatriots are tinged with shame and embarrassment and rarely express more than a murmur and a sigh. She wore Japanese clothing for most of the latter part of her life and wrote her correspondence with a calligraphy brush on old-fashioned scrolled letter paper. I do not think she did these things out of a foreign-raised woman's attraction to exotic Japanese things, but because in that time and in that situation, it seemed to her the reasonable and aesthetically sensible thing to do. Why should Japanese spend foolish sums of money on imitation Western clothing and other Western articles instead of the domestic products that were much easier to come by? That is to say, hers was an ethos based upon reasonable reflection.

She wanted Japanese women to learn to appreciate Western rationalism as she had learned it in America—not through easily attainable material objects and forms, but in its fundamental essence. Learning the English language, which would probably become a representative world language in the future, would be a good way for them to better understand the Western ideas behind the language. At the same time, it would lead to the possibility of a career in teaching English, economic independence, and a position in which they could express themselves. Umeko observed the social phenomena, applied scientific methods of synthesis and analysis, and came to a conclusion typical of her character.

Her letters to Adeline during the second half of 1888 frequently expressed her desire to study in America again. She asked Adeline to send catalogues of various women's colleges such and worried about the cost:

No. 8 Kioicho³
July 10, 1888

. . . As to coming to America to study . . . I think if I came again, I should enter some institution in the North for special branches, [such] as a normal school,⁴ to make the science of teaching a specialty and see how it is done in some of the large schools. . . . I want to find out what the expenses are at some of these institutions. Could you find out for me, and get me a catalogue of Smith College, or Wellesley, or some of these places, so I could see and think it over?

As to the idea of my coming to America making my return again irksome, that would be nonsense. . . . I want to come, because I want to study some more and fit myself better to be a teacher, not for pleasure. If I had the money I should decide.

October 15, 1888

. . . Our late principal Genera Otori quite encouraged me in my idea, but gave no more hope than help in expenses as much as salary. . . .

Around this time, Umeko was joined by Alice Bacon, who had come to Japan through her connection to Sutematsu and Umeko. She and Umeko decided to share the rent for the house of a foreign ministry official who had temporarily gone abroad. Alice Bacon was the daughter of the family with whom Sutematsu had boarded while she attended Vassar and the two were good friends. Umeko was now hearing about America in her

---

3 Where Umeko had recently set up house in preparation for an extended visit by Alice Bacon.

4 "Normal school" indicated a teacher training school, more often called a teacher-training college today. It was referred to as a "normal" school because it taught the norms of pedagogy.

conversations with Alice, and this must have prompted her to consider another course of study abroad in more concrete terms.

She had been in close contact with many girls after accepting a job at the Peeresses' School, and it is understandable that she should want to step back from national policy and educate the women of the future in a different way, by teaching them at a private school of her own. Japanese men apparently regarded the ideal of Japanese womanhood to be the placid, genteel princesses being nurtured at the Peeresses' School, although for entertainment these same men turned to geishas and prostitutes.

The majority of her students were forcibly married off while too young to awaken to their selfhood. Umeko writes again and again with much indignation about the way Japanese girls married at a very young age and were pushed into the innermost sanctuary of the house with the title of *okusama*—the common word for "wife" in Japanese that literally means "one who stays deep within." Women too poor to have inner sanctuaries to retire to existed exclusively as mothers, at the beck and call of their children and hounded by housework for the rest of their lives.

Umeko realized from her day-to-day experiences that women would have no say in anything until they gained economic independence. She was disgusted at the way men squandered money on prostitutes, but she also realized that the audacity of these professional women was based on a sort of financial independence that they possessed, because they could obtain money from a man by means of whatever natural talents they had. It was this astuteness that made them so fascinating to men. What was the difference between women who gained economic power by flirting promiscuously with all and sundry, and women who entered into advantageous marriages in order to enjoy stable lives under the protection of a single man? They were different, but both situations were unsatisfactory from a woman's point of view.

Umeko was naturally attracted to men and appreciated their power, so the position of women in Japan must have been a source of grief to her. She did not think that girls of the upper classes were worthy of being held up as models of behavior, but the general population was oblivious regarding the situation of women, and the women themselves had nothing to say for themselves. There was more to a woman's life than keeping house under a man's direction and being a mother who brought up children to his liking. Umeko's dream was for men and women to exchange ideas freely and to help each other, and she wanted to educate women who could speak out from a vantage point that was different from a man's, so that they could deal with new problems and build a future together.

Neither the Peeresses' School nor any other public school for women was educating women to that end. Umeko could not remain inactive when she thought about the next generation being brought up by women educated at such schools. Looking outward from Japan, she knew the situation might not be so rosy elsewhere either, but at least the world was in motion and exploring new possibilities.

The first thing Umeko did was to ask for specific advice from Mrs. Mary Morris, who lived in Philadelphia. The Morrises were an old, established family of the city and Umeko knew them from her Archer Institute days by way of Mr. and Mrs. Whitney, who were acquainted with Umeko's father Sen. Umeko had continued to correspond with Mrs. Morris after returning to Japan and frequently mentioned her name in letters to Adeline.

Mrs. Morris appears to have had great influence in intellectual circles on the east coast and she was also a Japanophile whose house was frequented by eminent Japanese. This is a tradition that has been kept up in her family, and even today, many Japanese continue to visit the Morris home.

Adeline, needless to say, loved Umeko like a daughter and wanted more than anything to have her back in America again. In order to help Umeko realize her plan, she began telling her friends that the little foreign girl she had brought up was now a beacon of hope for women's education in Japan, a country slated to become the leader of East Asia. Both Adeline and Mrs. Morris were soon thinking of Umeko's dream in their own terms.

Mrs. Morris was a friend of James E. Rhoads, president of a women's college that had recently been established by Quakers (a Christian denomination that arose in England in the seventeenth century) at Bryn Mawr, in the suburbs of Philadelphia. Learning of Umeko's desire to study abroad, she immediately recommended the young Asian woman to Rhoads. Rhoads assented at once and promised Umeko a tuition waiver as well as a room in the dormitory. On her side, Umeko obtained a two-year leave of absence from the Peeresses' School, maintaining her salary and position through the good offices of the school principal.

Why was Umeko so fortunate as to obtain assistance, from childhood on, from such a long series of capable people—Japanese and American, women and men? Charles and Adeline Lanman, Itō Hirobumi, Mori Arinori, Ōtori Keisuke and Nishimura Shigeki (successive principals of the Peeresses' School), Alice Bacon, Sutematsu, Shigeko, and the Morrises all did what they could to help her. Anna Hartshorne, mentioned in the first chapter of this book, eventually dedicated her whole life to the school that Umeko founded.

Umeko had many siblings and they and their families also helped her throughout her lifetime. The husband of her elder sister Kotoko, Ueno Eizaburō, was unstintingly generous with financial support when Umeko founded and then managed her school. From the time she was very young, Umeko cheerfully looked after her younger brothers and sisters, sleeping with them in the same room, taking care of their needs, and wholeheartedly enjoying the time she spent with them. This attitude extended beyond her own siblings. The episode about the princess of the Kujō family, recounted in an earlier chapter, is one example. Umeko often had girls in her own home, regardless of social class, and looked after them.

Human actions are invariably reciprocal. The fact that people around Umeko offered her so much help is an indication of how helpful she was to them, in ways both tangible and intangible. It also reflects her magnetism as a human being, and her abundant vitality. It seems to me that people around her responded to her presence and to the light in her eyes as a beacon of hope that promised humanity a brighter future on earth.

In fact, Umeko had very little ambition for herself. When she was invited to the great balls at Rokumeikan, she attended a few times, eyes wide open to see what there was to see, but turned coolly away from the ones that followed. "I have no intention of sacrificing other things to buy expensive Western costumes that are so hard to come by in Japan," was her attitude. "I have more important things to do and cannot spare the time."

She was neither an optimist nor a pessimist. She accepted things as they were, instinctively homed in on whatever path was open to her, and pursued it. The people she met along the way likewise followed their instincts in joining their strengths to hers as she forged ahead into the future.

In the same year that Umeko decided to return to America as a student, the Meiji Constitution, prepared over many years by Itō Hirobumi and others to declare Japan's birth as a new nation, was promulgated on February 11, 1889. Article 28 guaranteed citizens the freedom of religious belief.

A tragic event occurred on the very day of the promulgation. The minister of education, Mori Arinori, was assassinated. Umeko wrote in a letter to Adeline that the reported reason for the murder was that Mori had angered the Shinto priests of Ise Shrine by stepping into a sanctuary without removing his shoes and then pushing aside a sacred curtain with his walking stick. The assassin was cut down and killed on the spot. The emperor and the worship of imperial ancestors were sacred symbols for Japanese nationalism, she explained, and politics and religion were so deeply entangled that it was difficult to discover the real reason for the crime. Umeko worried about the impression that such an incident would make in foreign countries and whether it would damage Japan's position in negotiating a new treaty. Be that as it may, Umeko sailed from Yokohama six months later to resume her studies in America.

Umeko majored in biology at Bryn Mawr College. It seems to me that she chose this field because she thought of the study of humankind as being a branch of biology. As the daughter of Tsuda Sen, agriculturalist of the Meiji era, she had been interested in biology from an early age. She also had a strong natural inclination for science, and school records indicate that she always excelled in scientific subjects.

Darwin's *On the Origin of the Species* was published in 1859 and biology was enormously popular when Umeko was growing up. Her interest in natural selection is demonstrated in a letter cited earlier, where she mentioned some morning glory seeds she had sent to Adeline and asked her to observe how the colors change from generation to generation.

The founding of Bryn Mawr College was made possible by Joseph Wright Taylor, a Quaker physician from New Jersey. Taylor passed away in 1880 and left a will indicating that he felt the world was in need of a place where young women could be educated with the same advantages given to young men.

Dalton Hall, one of the few buildings on campus remaining from Umeko's time, has many labs and science-related reference rooms. Biology was regarded as an important field from the time of the school's founding. Umeko had various catalogues of women's colleges sent to her before she chose Bryn Mawr, and the decisive reasons for her choice may have been, aside from the offer of economic assistance, the emphasis on education for women equal to that of men, and the school's high regard for biology, a subject in which she was greatly interested.

Umeko's dormitory also still stands. The Bryn Mawr school catalogue includes a photo of Umeko in her dormitory room with her roommate, Anna Powers. The caption states that Miss Tsuda was a student from Japan and one of the first students from a foreign land to become famous.

The student who showed me around the campus was kind enough to let me peek into one of the dormitory rooms, which had a layout and general air that took me back for a moment to my own college dorm life more than thirty years earlier. Tsuda College's location in a wooded suburb of a big city, the choice of a secluded and distinctive environment in which to build its dormitories and lecture halls—the founder and her successors had obviously been thinking of Bryn Mawr when they built the school. The Bryn Mawr dormitory had single and double rooms, and the beds, desks, wardrobes, stacks of books, and notebooks all emitted the odor of young womanhood. The desktop computers reminded me that thirty years had passed and this made me sentimental, but I was dragged back to reality by the sight of male students lounging in the lobby, looking completely at home.

To reach Bryn Mawr, I had taken the Metroliner from New York to Philadelphia. I had been on the train twice before, respectively ten years and twenty years earlier. The scenery through the train window had changed very little—it still had a bleak, industrial look. But the new train had a rounded nose like an airplane and was better than the old one.

The train stopped in Newark before arriving in Philadelphia and I saw long row-houses that made me think of factories and concentration camps. They reminded me of scenes of England during the Industrial Revolution. People immigrated to the New World and built the same things they had in the old one, I mused. Another instance of people's thoughts crossing the ocean like sparks of fire.

The train passed through a tunnel and arrived at 30th Street Station. The station had an extravagantly high ceiling supported by Grecian columns and was an impressive structure worthy of the major station it had no doubt once been, but now it had a forlorn air, with dining possibilities limited to cafeterias and hamburger shops. Still, it looked neat and well maintained. I walked through an arcaded passageway and reached the platform for the Paoli Line. Pigeon droppings dotted the platform and it had a roof supported by steel girders with many rivets. An elderly couple was waiting for the train and they told me that the Paoli Line dated back to before the Civil War and was part of Pennsylvania's oldest railway system.

The train passed through suburban residential areas with beautiful fall colors. Some of the stations looked as if they had been there since the train began running. They had low-lying platforms and the tranquil air typical to local branch lines. The train carriages had rows of two and three seats, just like the Japanese Shinkansen bullet train. A conductor came by to check my ticket, which he stuck on the back of the seat in front of me and took away again before I got off.

Bryn Mawr College is located a few hundred meters from the small station. The trees were bright with autumn leaves and women students walked here and there, along with a scattering of male students. I had letters of introduction from Ōtsuka Yuriko, former president of Tsuda College, and Uchida Michiko, who was a few years ahead of me when I was at Tsuda and who is now a professor there, so I was invited to stay at Windom House, a guesthouse on campus. Windom House was an eighteenth century farmhouse purchased by the college in 1926 and turned out to be a lovely old-fashioned building with walls fifty centimeters thick. The furniture was also antique and had been collected by Carey Thomas, first dean of the college and its second president.

Let me tell you briefly about Carey Thomas, a pioneer in feminism. She was dean at Bryn Mawr when Umeko studied there, but became president in 1894. Carey helped and advised Umeko when she sent students to Bryn Mawr from Japan using the proceeds of the scholarship fund that she established during her time at Bryn Mawr with the assistance of Mrs. Morris.

Carey was born to a Quaker family and graduated from Cornell University in 1875 with outstanding marks. Women were not allowed to attend graduate schools in those days, but Johns Hopkins University made a special exception to accept her. She was not permitted to attend classes with her male colleagues, however, and had to sit behind a curtain to hear the lectures. Dissatisfied with the state of her education, she decided that she wanted to study at a German university, which was what ambitious young scholars aspired to do back then.

Carey's father was violently opposed to the plan, but her mother was sympathetic and came up with a strategy: "We will cry," she said. After mother and daughter cried all through a day and a night, the father succumbed, and Carey went to Leipzig University to study. She did excellent work for three years, but the university did not award degrees to women. She was subsequently accepted at Zurich University, where she became the first woman to earn a Ph.D.

After this, Carey became a trailblazing leader of women's education. She opened the way for women to go to Europe to study, and also for women who wanted to study medicine. She set up summer schools for women who worked in industry, demanded political and economic rights for women, and is regarded today as a forerunner of the feminist movement.

Umeko's selection of Bryn Mawr for her studies was a twist of fortune that resulted in connecting various threads of destiny in an inscrutable way. Umeko's initial plan before leaving Japan had been a two-year course of study, but she was allowed an extension for a third year, ostensibly to continue her investigation of women's education in America. She spent six months at Oswego Teacher's Training School, located on the southeastern shore of Lake Ontario, studying pedagogical methods. (The school was famous for introducing the Pestalozzi method[5] to the U.S.)

---

5 An educational method developed by Swiss educator Johann Pestalozzi (1746–1827) that stresses the development of all aspects of a person, including the intellectual, the emotional, and the physical.

During these three years, Umeko often met with Alice Bacon, who had returned to America somewhat after her, and the two discussed *Japanese Girls and Women*, the book that Alice was working on at the time. Alice and Umeko carefully considered Japanese women of different classes and began to envision specific plans for the future women of Japan. Umeko asked Alice to help her when she founded a private school, and years later, Alice kept her promise by rushing to Umeko's side when she heard that the school would open and by teaching there for two years without compensation.

Umeko also became acquainted with Anna Hartshorne while she was at Bryn Mawr. Anna later came to Japan, and as the two came to know each other better, she made a similar promise to help Umeko. She took over from Alice Bacon and devoted herself to Umeko and the school for many years afterwards. Umeko was like a giant star, with gravity strong enough to draw every nearby star into her orbit.

The day I visited, an alumnae meeting was taking place in the dining room of Windom House and a great many elderly ladies were in attendance. A luncheon of refined home-style cooking was served to us in a friendly manner. I was feeling relieved that the gathering was very sedate despite its large size, when a young woman came up to me and introduced herself as the president's secretary. The president was unfortunately out of town for a conference, she said, but everyone would do what they could for me, as Bryn Mawr and Tsuda College had enjoyed a very close relationship since Umeko's time.

Indeed, a woman who had been a classmate of Uchida Michiko's at Bryn Mawr was now working in the university library, and she made copies for me of letters written by Tsuda Umeko to Carey Thomas, and also gave me some information on the school's history. Everywhere I went, I was treated like an old friend.

A hundred years ago, through the circle of connections that radiated from this school, Tsuda Umeko, in the position of a student, amassed a fund of 8,000 dollars with the help of Mrs. Morris. This became the scholarship that permitted one woman student every few years to study in America for four years. Throughout her life, Umeko had an amazing talent for establishing funds like this for educational purposes, including the founding of her own school. She was exceptionally frugal with regard to her own needs, and used all the money she collected for the education of young women. This was precisely why so many donations came her way.

Twenty-five women studied abroad on what was called the American Scholarship for Japanese Women. They include educators like Matsuda Michiko, head of Dōshisha Women's College, Kawai Michiko, head of Keisen Jogakuen (Keisen Girls' School), Suzuki Utako, professor at Gakushūin Girls' School, Hoshino Ai, president of Tsuda College, Fujita Taki, also a Tsuda president, and others. Professor Uchida Michiko of Tsuda University, whom I frequently call upon these days to ask questions related to this book and who unfailingly responds with kindness, went to Bryn Mawr on the scholarship while I was a student at Tsuda College.

Umeko worked as an assistant to biologist T. H. Morgan while she was at Bryn Mawr and co-authored a paper with him regarding the genesis of frogs' eggs. He encouraged her to remain at the college to continue her research—an invitation that would have sorely tempted any student, especially a foreign one, in that day. But Umeko considered the education of Japanese women to be her mission, and returned to the Peeresses' School with the 8,000-dollar scholarship as a coming-home present.

I wonder about Umeko's thoughts as she watched frog-egg cells dividing under her microscope. The mystery of life reproducing itself as the cells divided and redivided must have connected in her mind to the fundraising she undertook for the sake of younger women and to the future she envisioned for them. If she had stayed on at the college to work in biology as she was recommended to do, she might have become a world-class biologist. Even after she returned to Japan, she always had new publications in biology close at hand, indicating the depth of her interest in the field.

Bryn Mawr College was established in 1885 as a groundbreaking institution for women's education. Following the wishes of its founder, women were given the opportunity to pursue academic scholarship in fields such as Greek, mathematics, and philosophy, which had previously been confined to men. Curriculum standards were equal to those of Oxford, Yale, and Princeton.

Bryn Mawr is also a small college that can offer its students special guidance to a degree not always possible at larger schools. And when education faces new and important problems, the school is proud of its tradition of not clinging to old habits, but of making brave new decisions. More than anything else, it claims to realize the ideal of an education that respects individuality.

To avoid any narrow-mindedness or exclusivity, which often comes with smallness, Bryn Mawr conducts numerous cooperative programs with nearby Haverford College and Pennsylvania University. Students of those institutions may attend lectures without paying extra tuition and can also earn credits. Of the several dormitories, some are co-ed and some for women only.

At the same time, Bryn Mawr is one of the few well-known private colleges in America that have remained a women's college (although the graduate school is coeducational). The faculty, on the other hand, is half men and half women. Men and women are equally active in all academic fields and on the board of directors. The present head of the board,[6] Mary McPherson, says the presence of male students in Bryn Mawr's classrooms

---

6   That is, in 1990, when the present volume was first published in Japan.

and on campus does not detract from the school's identity as a women's college. Rather, she says, it underscores that character.

One of the traits of a small private college is that many of the people who work there are alumnae and have personal ties to the school. The school is pervaded by rationalism, a predominant feature of American civilization (although this is somewhat in question these days), but the friendly courtesy, the rules, the manners of self-expression, and the confident bearing of people on campus seem to be grounded on personal relationships.

There is a story at Bryn Mawr that Carey Thomas, once regarded as one of the leading intellectual women of America, was more pleased than by any other words of praise when a Bryn Mawr graduate said to her: "I've forgotten everything else I learned at Bryn Mawr, but I will never forget the one thing you always said when you stood up and spoke to us at chapel every morning. You said, 'Believe in woman.'"

FOUNDING

From a letter to Mrs. Morris:

December 28, 1899

I have been wanting to write you especially of late to tell you that at the end of the present school year, I am going to ask to resign from my work in the Peeresses' School, and take up the school work about which I talked to you last summer.[1] You know how much I have wanted to do this . . . in spite of the honor that there is in teaching the nobility. My plan is to offer a few higher courses of study, English being made a special feature and students prepared for our government examinations for teachers. At present there are *no* private schools that offer any courses of study to prepare for these examinations and consequently very few women apply for the certificate. The government normal school for women gives a course of study which is very good, and which prepares teachers for the schools,[2] but those who can get the vacancies are few, and there are obligations after graduation and restrictions that prevent many from applying. I am very anxious to do what I can to help the higher education of women and from henceforth want to put myself in that line of work.

Miss Alice Bacon, now of Hampton, Va., will help me in this work and as she is well known in Japan her name will be a great help.

As you may know, tuition fees in all schools here are almost nominal, and I can not expect much pay from the students which will go

---

1   Umeko went to America in 1898 to attend the International Congress of the Federation of Women's Clubs in Denver, Colorado, as the Japanese delegate. She extended her trip to visit Europe, and spent extra time in America to visit Adeline and acquaintances from her Bryn Mawr years.

2   The curriculum however did not include English.

to support the institution. Altho' I shall give up my salary from the government, I do not even expect that my own support will come from the work, as it would be impossible to expect it. I want to try the experiment for five years, and if at the end of that time, it is successful to try and put the school on a good foundation. . . .

I shall, however, in any case have to have about three or four thousand dollars to get a suitable house and grounds to start the work in, and without that I feel it is impossible for me to do anything. I am now planning ahead from this time to see what can be done before the summer time towards this.

I am sure you know my heart is in this work, for I have talked it over with you, and now I write to ask your help to tell me what I can do towards getting this amount to start the school. Perhaps the members of our scholarship committee would feel interested in the plans of this work, for my desire is that our students at Bryn Mawr may return and work with us there, and I am sure the school would open a new field of work. . . .

I have already written Miss M. Carey Thomas about this. . . . and I am hoping and praying that the way may open out. While I am in the government school, I am not free in any way to carry out my own ideas of education. Of cource [sic], it is all right that you and my other friends should know of my plans and my desires to carry out this work and to resign from the Peeresses' School, but as the fact of my resignation can not be carried out now, will you please be careful that the news does not come back to Japan. . . . I should dislike to have exaggerated reports and rumors of my work get abroad and Tokyo is a very dreadful place for gossip. . . .[3]

---

3 *Tsuda Umeko bunsho* [Writings of Tsuda Umeko], 383–85.

Umeko had decided at last that the time was ripe to establish a private school. It had taken many years, and more than a dozen had passed since she began teaching at the Peeresses' School. But the idea was there, nascent, from the time she first became aware of the world, or in any case from the age of seven, when it was impressed on her young mind that her mission was to learn about foreign lands for the sake of the future of Japanese women. This idea had gestated and ripened and was finally in a state of fermentation. Umeko was thirty-six years old when she made the decision to found a school.

My mind goes back to my own long road as a writer. I also carried the thought in my mind from as far back as I can remember. From the time I learned to read and sensed the presence of living people behind the words, even if it was just a few lines in a children's picture book, I sensed that I would someday be a person who wrote such stories.

Many people other than Umeko and myself begin to dream about their future from a very young age, and I have seen many cases where they actually follow a path similar to the one they envisioned. I was also thirty-six when I wrote *Three Crabs*,[4] but I had been writing manuscripts in my spare time for more than twenty years before that. It seems to me that it was my destiny to become a writer, and that I could not have followed any other path.

As indicated in Umeko's letter to Mrs Morris, she had spoken of her plan to only a chosen few, and did not mention the school in any of her letters to Adeline around that time. It seems odd that she did not touch on her momentous decision in the voluminous letters that she wrote to Adeline nearly every week, but perhaps because the plan was becoming concrete, she was concerned that the Lanmans, who had close links to Japanese diplomatic circles, might let something slip to the Japanese side. Or, she may have

---

4   Ōba's debut novel: *Sanbiki no kani* [Three Crabs] (Tokyo: Kōdansha, 1968).

wanted to keep them from worrying about the financial aspects of the project. The Lanmans looked upon Umeko as a daughter and would have spared no effort in helping her to realize her long-cherished dream. Nevertheless, before long, her plans became public and people were duly astonished.

Umeko had a professorial position at the Peeresses' School with an annual salary of 800 yen, which in those days was a privileged and cutting-edge position for a woman of thirty-six. A list of wages in that era, compiled by the magazine *Shūkan Asahi*,[5] informs us that a member of the National Diet earned two thousand yen per annum in 1899, while a manual laborer was paid a national average of thirty-seven *sen* (0.37 yen) per diem in 1900. Anyone with common sense would naturally wonder why she would embark on such a foolhardy project.

On July 20, 1900, Umeko applied to Tokyo prefecture for permission to establish a private school called Joshi Eigaku Juku (Women's School for English Studies) and received approval on the 26th of that month. As recounted in Chapter 8, her old friend Alice Bacon had come to Japan in the spring to assist her, and Watanabe Mitsuko, Suzuki Utako, and Sakurai Hikoichirō joined the enterprise.

Watanabe Mitsuko was a niece of Umeko's cousin, Watanabe Masako. (Masako was working at the Peeresses' School when Umeko began teaching there in 1885, and the two women rented a house together in Akasaka Tango-chō.) Alice Bacon came to Japan in 1889, and she took the four-year-old Mitsuko back with her to America and brought her up. The girl was now grown up and accompanied Alice to Japan when the school was founded so they could help Umeko together.

---

5 *Nedan no Meiji, Taishō, Shōwa fūzoku-shi* [History of Prices in the Meiji, Taishō, and Shōwa Eras], ed. Shūkan Asahi (Tokyo: Asahi Shimbunsha, 1981–82). The figures are taken from various tables scattered throughout the three volumes.

Suzuki Utako was a recipient of the American Scholarship for Japanese Women that Umeko had established while she was a student at Bryn Mawr, with the help of Mrs. Morris. Umeko returned to Japan from her studies at Bryn Mawr in 1892 and resumed teaching at the Peeresses' School in September of that year. Utako was one of several girls who lived with her during this time. Umeko always had girls in her home and looked after their needs, and when these girls became adults, they often returned to help her. She continued to teach at the school for eight years after her return, perhaps from a feeling of obligation to the institution that had allowed her to study in America again. Once she felt that she had fulfilled her obligation, she went on to establish her own school.

Sakurai Hikoichirō had visions for women's education from early on and taught at Meiji Girls' School. Umeko taught higher-level students at Meiji Girls' School around 1894–1895 while she was still working at the Peeresses' School, which is probably where the two became acquainted. Sakurai is said to have suggested the name "Joshi Eigaku Juku," and it was he who managed the business side of establishing the new school. Iwamoto Yoshiharu, Nitobe Inazō, and others presented a series of enthusiastic and celebratory lectures in support of Umeko's new project.[6] Ōyama Sutematsu took on the role of adviser and Ueno Eizaburō (the businessman who was married to Umeko's sister Kotoko) generously provided financial support.

In sum, countless people supported Umeko, both in spirit and materially, throughout her lifetime. I have already remarked on her uncanny ability to attract sympathetic and supportive individuals.

Joshi Eigaku Juku opened its doors to students on September 14, 1900. The building was an ordinary Japanese house located at 15 Ichiban-chō,

---

6 Iwamoto Yoshiharu (1863–1942) was an early advocate of women's education and one of the founders of Meiji Girls' School. Nitobe Inazō (1862–1933) was a leading intellectual of the era who earned degrees in both the U.S. and Germany. After returning to Japan, Nitobe embarked on a prolific career as an agricultural economist, writer, educator, diplomat, and politician.

Joshi Eigaku Juku was launched in an ordinary house with just ten students. (Photographed on March 29, 1901)

Photo courtesy of Tsuda University.

Kōjimachi, and there were just ten students. Each student was taught according to her academic ability by Umeko, Alice Bacon, Suzuki Utako, and others, often by private tutoring. The annual budget for the school was listed as follows:[7]

Revenue: Tuition from thirty students: 720 yen
              Boarding fees for five dormitory students: 1,080 yen
              Dormitory fees for the same: 225 yen
              Total: 2,025 yen
Expenditure: Salaries for teachers: 720 yen
              Boarding costs: 1,080 yen
              Other: 225 yen
              Total: 2,025 yen

This budget indicates that most of the teachers were teaching for almost nothing. In fact, Umeko and Alice received no salary at all. In the first

7   Yamazaki, *Tsuda Umeko*, 182–83.

years (until 1904, when the school was recognized as a vocational school), Umeko supported herself by teaching classes at Tokyo Women's Higher Normal School (precursor of Ochanomizu University) and by tutoring members of the Yamashina-no-miya and Iwasaki families. Alice Bacon taught at the Peeresses' School in addition to Joshi Eigaku Juku and lived on that income, and she also paid rent for her private quarters in the school building as a tribute to her long friendship with Umeko.

For the opening ceremony of the school, Umeko prepared a speech in English but actually spoke in Japanese. However, a resumé of the original English text was published in the October 1900 edition of *Shin Eigo* (The Present English), a magazine for students of English.

> During the ten years or more that I have been in educational work, there is one thing which has especially impressed me, in regard to education. It is this—true education does not depend on the school buildings, apparatus, and other accessories, and while fine class rooms, books, and other helps are not to be despised but to be made as perfect as possible, yet these material objects, or even any one fixed method or system of work are far from comparison with other and more essential things of a school. I mean by this, the qualifications of the teachers and pupils, and the spirit in which they pursue their work. It seems to me quite possible therefore to carry on the true work of education, even with greater restricted means, if teachers and pupils have with them the true spirit of work.
>
> Another thing which has impressed me is the difficulty in large schools of teaching a great number of pupils at once. It is possible to impart a certain amount of knowledge at one time to a large class, but in true education, each one ought to be dealt with as a separate individual, for we know that one's mental and moral characteristics vary as do the faces of each one of us. . . .

Having these thoughts in mind, I have been wanting to have a limited number of pupils under me in my own school, to see what I could do for them in their education, for I felt that by earnest effort, much could be done, even though with limited means, and little help.

Through a strange fortune, I was sent abroad for study while very young. On my return it was my wish to do what I could with my limited ability towards the education of our girls, to give to others what I had been enabled to learn. At the time of my return, the state of society was different from the present. There was little opportunity to work for the higher education of our women, and not much chance for the pupils to make practical use of such training even if received. Lately, however, much progress has been made for our women, and as you know, high schools for girls are yearly increasing. The Educational Department admits women to its examinations for the High School teacher's certificate. It has been a matter of regret to me that with this opening for women-teachers, so few have been able to pass the examinations, and it is my desire to be able to help in this school those who wish the English teacher's certificate. This is one of the objects of our three year's course. . . .

In pursuing a special course of study, one is apt to become narrow. In learning one thing well, we are apt to lose our hold of other things. In taking this special English course, and while endeavoring to perfect yourselves in this branch, do not neglect other things, which go to make up the complete women; endeavor daily to keep yourselves informed of general matters, and to be in touch with other lines of work. . . .

There is one thing that I must warn you as student to be careful about. This school is the first of its kind in making a specialty of its higher courses of study. We may be criticized on many points. Perhaps some of these may not be of much importance, but even then, if such criticism impede the progress of the higher education for women, it would be a matter of great regret to all of us. And criticism will mostly come, not so much on our courses of study or methods of work, but on points which simply require a little care and thoughtfulness on your part . . . the language you use, your manner in intercourse with others—your attention to the details of our etiquette. So I ask you not in any way to make yourselves conspicuous or to seem forward, but be always gentle, submissive and courteous as have always been our women in the past. . . .[8]

Yamazaki Takako has an interesting opinion as to why this speech was given in Japanese.

There remains some doubt as to why Umeko gave this speech in Japanese, because on all subsequent public occasions such as ceremonies, she always spoke in English. Not only documents, but her letters and diaries are all in English. She was not unable to speak Japanese, but for Umeko, English was the language in which she could express her thoughts with freedom and confidence. Yet, historical documents of the school and Umeko's biography are in agreement that her opening address was "in Japanese." A memoir of a student who was present at the ceremony (Okuyama Shizuka) also states that she spoke in Japanese. Considering the matter, one realizes that if Umeko had spoken English on the day of the school's opening, hardly any of the students would have understood her. On the day the school took its first step into the world, Umeko did not utter any of the stock phrases usually spoken on such occasions. That she spoke at length in Japanese, of matters worthy of deep consideration, seems to me a reflection of her keen resolve.[9]

8 *Shin Eigo* [The Present English], vol. 12 (Tokyo: Shineigosha, 1900), 1–3.
9 Yamazaki, *Tsuda Umeko*, 190.

I have quoted verbatim from Umeko's speech to illustrate this keen resolve and her manner of expressing it. Her true purpose in founding the school, in view of the state of the world at the time, was to give Japanese women the tool of English as a way to open their eyes, to give them a place to work, to give them some say in society, and to draw them up to an equal status with men.

Umeko spoke the following words in the course of her effort, aided by Mrs. Morris, to raise the funds necessary to give Japanese women the opportunity to study in America.

> While I have been in this country, the one thing which has struck me particularly, and filled me with admiration is the position American women hold . . . In Japan there has never been any great prejudice against women such as we find in so many countries of the East . . . [but] the introduction of the doctrines of Confucius from China, and the religion of Buddha from India have all had their blighting influence. . . . Confucius says a woman's duty is obedience, and her judgment must never be trusted. The so-called "three obediences" are—when young to her father, when married to her husband, when a widow to her son.
>
> Happily, the influence of Buddha and Confucius is growing, year by year, less powerful in Japan, and we are hoping that Christianity will fill the void. . . . People have marvelled at Japan passing through centuries of change in a few years, and ending with a constitutional monarchy barely twenty-five years after the breaking down of the feudal system. It is because the Japanese people have wished to be on a level with other nations, to take equal rank with the countries of Europe and America. It is for this they have worked, and to a certain degree I think I may say they have succeeded, for Japan now has a constitutional government and a parliament of her people. But with

all these advances for the nation, and much progress for the men, no corresponding advantages have been given to the women. . . .

I had hoped that this time of great change when so much of the old has been discarded would prove a turning point in the history of the women. . . . Women must have their rights regarded and be an influence for good in society. . . .

I want to speak of the need of education for women of the upper classes. We should expect them to have the greatest influence. Yet they are the ones who are the most backward in the present progressive movement. Living in their secluded homes, they are the hardest to be reached by Christian missionaries, or by the advocates of the new education, who, like myself, believe that woman has a more serious part to play in the world than to be a mere ornament for the home, or plaything for the men. . . .

The wives of the middle classes have their household duties, and the care of their children, and they see, too, something of the world outside. But the wives of the wealthy have not any occupation and responsibility. . . .

As we go down the social scale, the difference between men and women becomes less, but it is only in the poorest class that there seems absolute equality. In the middle class there is a lack of real sympathy between men and women due to difference in training and education.

When I returned home after my first visit to America . . . a woman could hold no property in her own name, and her identity was merged in that of father, husband, or some male relative. Hence there was an utter lack of independent spirit. . . . To be sure, a woman could obtain a divorce from her husband, but this meant an equal dependence on some one else, as well as the loss of her own children, and most women would endure almost anything from their husbands rather than ask for a separation. . . .

The indifference to the position and education of women began to disappear about six or seven years ago. Along with many other innovations, people began to talk of helping and elevating the women.... [But] women, especially among those of the higher classes ... cannot be reached by foreign ladies. ... They are a conservative class, the ladies pay more attention to little details of etiquette which are so hard for a foreigner to learn, and above all, there is a lack of a common tongue. A well educated, cultivated, native woman, even though she is herself not of high rank, can as a teacher find her way to the homes of this exclusive class, and through education, the lesson of Christianity could be taught. Such well educated teachers would have a great influence in the country.

The plan which I have is this, I desire that a permanent scholarship fund be raised, the interest of which would enable a Japanese woman to take a four years' course of study in one of your institutions. It would be open to all Japanese women ... a free gift from American ladies, to show the interest which has been taken in them, and the high value attached by American ladies to education. ... I feel that such a scholarship offered in this way, directly to the Japanese would have a very great influence, and would help to do away with the feeling now so prevalent in Japan that higher education is antagonistic to Christianity.[10]

In 1898, two years before the founding of Joshi Eigaku Juku, Tsuda Umeko attended the International Congress of the Federation of Women's Clubs in Denver, Colorado, as the Japanese delegate. In her presentation at the conference, which was reported in American newspapers and drew a wide response, she stated with confidence that the Japanese women she was

---

10 *Tsuda Umeko bunsho*, 19–27. The speech was presented in Philadelphia while she was a student at Bryn Mawr.

educating would soon be helping the women of other Asian nations to build a future society where men and women assisted one another.

Umeko had a Christian sense of mission, and she felt that as she was on the way to achieving her own dream with the help of American women, she was obliged, in the future, to lend a hand to the poor women of other Asian nations, who were leading even more downtrodden lives than Japanese women. Umeko looked upon the morality and ethics of Christianity from the viewpoint of a woman, and in comparing them to the morality and ethics of Confucianism and other systems of thought.

While I am on the subject of Umeko's Christian faith, let me mention a letter written by Uchimura Kanzō[11] that touches on the link between Christianity in Japan and American Puritanism. Professor Uchida Michiko of Tsuda University was kind enough to send me a photocopy of this letter, which was addressed to the family of Umeko's great supporter Mrs. Morris and sent to Philadelphia when Mrs. Morris passed away. Uchida (who was a recipient of the scholarship set up by Umeko with Mrs. Morris's help) often visited the home of Mrs. Morris's granddaughter, Mrs. McCoy, when she was a student at Bryn Mawr. She encountered the letter from Uchimura Kanzō in the course of one of these visits.

The Morrises had many Japanese friends who visited them, including men like Uchimura Kanzō, Noguchi Hideyo, Arishima Takeo, and Niijima Jō. Uchimura appears to have been particularly close to Mrs. Morris, and writes in the letter that Mrs. Morris was like a mother to him during the three and a half years that he spent in America, and that she was supportive and actively participated in his Christian activities. She often said to Uchimura, "Why, you're practically a Quaker!" Uchimura wrote regretfully that it was not "You are a real Quaker!" Uchimura added that people often

---

11 Uchimura Kanzō (1861–1930) was a well-known writer, Christian evangelist, and founder of the Nonchurch Movement of the Meiji and Taishō eras.

said of him that he was influenced by the Quakers, but that it was actually the influence of Mary Morris.

I read and reread this short letter and decided that there is a similarity between Umeko's feelings for Christianity and the link between Uchimura's faith and Mrs. Morris. Mrs. Morris was not the only one to exert such an influence. Umeko had numerous soul mates from her long years in the United States, beginning with Charles and Adeline Lanman, who shared her hopes and helped her to build a future for what they saw as their common humanity. It was their influence that led her to become a Christian. Her faith was based not so much on doctrine as on the very personal and human voices that spoke the doctrine to her.

Prior to the opening ceremony of Joshi Eigaku Juku, Umeko wrote the following lines to Carey Thomas (who had become president of Bryn Mawr College) in a letter dated August 9, 1900.

. . . In resigning from the court school, I gave up my official title and rank, and yet I felt that my long connection of over ten years with a government school, would give me influence to begin a new thing on my own responsibility. It has been a more difficult thing to leave the school than anyone in democratic America could realize, but I have been able to do so, I think, honorably. I do not feel, however, that I can, for two or three years yet, appeal to my Japanese acquaintances for help for my own plans. It would be unwise to do so at present, and after all, I do not ask now for more than a start, as the beginning is to be a small one. However, I shall offer higher courses of study in the three years' work to be pursued, and the students are to be drawn from graduates of the government High and Normal Schools. Preparation will be given for the government examinations in English, and it will be a higher course of study than any hitherto offered in the private schools in Japan.

I have now all things in readiness, official permission to open, our circulars are out, and there is a house in an excellent situation, which I am now securing. Mrs. Morris writes that she will forward the $2000 collected last Spring, towards the $4000 originally asked for, and hopes that more may be obtained in the early fall. The house is costing me $6000, not including furnishing, repairs etc., but I am willing to get this by a loan on the property, if the remainder of the $4000 could be obtained for me before December. It seems very hard to ask for help for anything as far away as this work is, but my desire to begin and carry this new line of work successfully urges me on to write and ask if the Committee could guarantee me the rest of the $4000. I still have $2000 to carry and all the other expenses. Property has gone up tremendously the last few years, but I am getting this at a very great bargain, and there is absolutely no risk of loss on it, as my business advisors assure me.

Miss Bacon & I expect to begin work, Sept 1st, and we are very encouraged by the prospects, as the present seems a most favorable time.

Excuse this long letter, but I wished to lay the situation before you [to] ask your help. . . . [12]

No doubt because Umeko was so completely without self-interest, this surprisingly direct plea for assistance had the power to move the reader. Umeko had been well liked at Bryn Mawr, and she had subsequently built up a good reputation for herself in many parts of the world. Those must have been the foundations she built on, because she received astoundingly generous donations from her friends in America. Half a year later, she had enough money from the committee in Philadelphia to purchase the former residence of Marquis Daigo Tadaosa at 41 Motozono-chō, 1 chōme.

---

12 *Tsuda Umeko bunsho*, 389–91.

In March 1901, the school had over thirty students; in 1907, it had 140. It had done very little in the way of advertising itself, but the name of Joshi Eigaku Juku spread by word of mouth throughout the country, and enlightened young women with dreams for a better future knocked on Umeko's door. They were reportedly astonished at the school's complete lack of stylishness and the unpretentious air of both Umeko and the whole institution.

In 1904, the school was certified as a vocational school, and from 1905, graduates were exempted from taking the teacher's certificate examination. This meant that graduates of Joshi Eigaku Juku were the first women in Japan to be awarded a privilege toward gaining employment as English teachers. When the school was certified as a vocational school, Umeko began for the first time to receive a monthly salary of twenty-five yen.

Umeko bore the financial burden of managing a continuously growing school for the rest of her life. She depended a great deal on contributions from sponsors in both America and Japan, and wrote a prodigious number of letters. Some of the letters have been cited in this book, but it is said that she was sometimes obliged to write as many as three hundred letters a month.

Umeko's father Tsuda Sen was apparently the first person to give his unreserved blessing to her idea of establishing a school. It seems certain that much of Umeko's innate ability and character came to her through her father.

> Sen was moved by Umeko's justification of her cause. It made him happy to think of his daughter standing tall as a pioneer of women's higher education. . . . His interest and passion for education can be surmised from his founding of Gakunōsha, a school for agriculture. His interest in women's education can be understood from his participation in the founding of Aoyama Girls' School and Friends Girls'

School. At the same time, he was keenly aware of the difficulty of managing a private school. He worried about the future, but when he realized that his daughter was determined to take this path, even at the cost of throwing away her professorship [at the Peeresses' School and the Women's Higher Normal School], he felt he must assent.[13]

. . . In public life, Sen was a pioneer of the Christian community and distinguished himself in social enterprise, but his private life was a troubled one. Sen [and his wife Hatsuko] had five sons and seven daughters, but the eldest son Motochika passed away at the age of thirty-five (in 1901), his third daughter Fukiko at twenty-one, and three others in infancy. Sen had another son with a maid. Hatsuko was extremely upset about this, and Umeko, who was fastidious about such things, refused to meet the half-brother who had taken his mother's family name (Kaneko). However, when the boy grew up and became a member of society, and perhaps because her feelings had mellowed, she eventually acknowledged him as her brother. Sen was not a duplicitous man who kept past offences hidden away in dark corners. In fact, he had a tendency to passionately repent his sins in public, which meant that many people knew the facts.

Sen and Hatsuko retired to Kamakura, and Umeko recalled that they lived quietly, Sen listening to Hatsuko play the *koto* and the two playing the board game *go* together. Hatsuko passed away at the age of sixty-two.[14]

Sen had died a year earlier, in 1908. He was seventy-one and breathed his last on a train on the Yokosuka Line. He was bringing laurel trees from

13 Yoshikawa, *Tsuda Umeko den*, 241.
14 Yamazaki, *Tsuda Umeko*, 228–29.

his old house in Tokyo, intending to replant them in the gardens of his house and church in Kamakura. The trees arrived in his name at Kamakura Station but the owner did not.

As I write this book, many people have been sending me or introducing me to a great deal of fascinating material. Suitō Setsuko, an editor at the publishing house Shinchōsha, told me about an interview-based article featuring a woman named Okamura Shinako (or Shina), who was a member of the fifth graduating class of Joshi Eigaku Juku but whose life took her away from the school entirely.

The interviewer was Murakami Yumiko, a freelance writer living in the U.S. at the time of the interview (1981). Okamura Shina was living in a Los Angeles nursing home for Japanese-Americans and was just short of her hundredth birthday. Murakami interviewed her in weekly one-hour sessions during the summer and autumn of 1981. The interview was conducted in Japanese and later edited by Murakami, who kept to Okamoto's own choice of words where possible, including her occasional use of English.

Okamura was personally tutored as a young woman by Tsuda Umeko. Her words bring Umeko to life so effectively that I will quote her at great length. The article was sent to Tsuda University by Murakami for the "Words from Alumnae" section of the second volume of the university's *Oral History Series.*[15]

Okamura Shina was born in Kobe in 1882 (the year eighteen-year-old Umeko returned to Japan after eleven years in America) as the daughter of Okamura Tōbei.

The following paragraphs are excerpts from the interview that relate to Umeko and Joshi Eigaku Juku:

---

15 Murakami Yumiko, "Okamoto Shinako," *Sotsugyōsei ni kiku* [Words from Alumnae], no. 5 (part of the *Oral History Series,* Vol. 2 [1982], published by Tsuda College), 6–18.

I'm almost one hundred—it's embarrassing. But I can't help it (laughs). It's nice—on my last birthday, my son and his wife came together (from the East). But one hundred is a problem, not something to celebrate. It's embarrassing.

. . . I forget everyday things so quickly. But I remember the past very clearly. . . .

I finished elementary school, but they didn't have girls' secondary schools yet, so I learned to sew and serve tea and arrange flowers. All I did was practice to be a wife.

Shina was married in 1899, at the age of seventeen.

My husband was a distant relative. We were together every day from the time I was fifteen or sixteen, so naturally we liked each other and we were married. My husband was two years older than me, I think.

He finished middle school and was adopted by his uncle. Then he went from a commercial school in Kobe to Hitotsubashi Higher Commercial School (in Tokyo) and graduated in 1904.

We were married in Kobe and moved to Tokyo. My husband was still studying at the Higher Commercial School, you know, and he thought I needed to know English (because he had a plan to come to America). So we talked it over, and I went to Joshi Eigaku Juku. . . .

We both went to school, renting a room and preparing our own meals. We lived in lots of places, but one of them was on the second floor of a saké shop—it was called Mikawaya and located near Ichigaya-mitsuke. Lots of shops in Tokyo sold prepared dishes, so we would buy things like *tsukudani*[16] and make miso soup and have that.

---

16 A meat, fish, or vegetable dish simmered in a strong broth of soy sauce and sweetening to make it highly preservable.

But then I became pregnant in 1903. I couldn't go to school any more, you see, so I went home to Kobe and on February 29, 1904, I had a baby, but it was a stillbirth—my baby was born dead. However, because of that, I went back to school. . . .

That year (1904), my husband graduated from the Higher Commercial School and came here (to America). My baby had died, so I went back to school, and Tsuda-sensei let me live in her house.

I was the only one there in her house, who saw her everyday life, learning from her. It was a big honor. I was the only one with her in the same house for two years, every day. . . . O-shina-san, o-shi-na-san—she used to call me. I can never forget what she did for me. She was a wonderful person. I was there when she was working so hard for women's education.

The school was in Kōjimachi, and it was really a "juku"—a little school—like the temple schools they used to have. This is when it was just begun and it was so very small. Only five or six students, when they called it Joshi Eigaku Juku. I was married, so I was the oldest of the students. It was a school for English and everything was in English, and most of the students came from the prefectures and they were graduates of girls' schools. I only finished elementary school, but I studied at the Tsuda school.

My English was very basic. But I had learned a little bit. Back then, even in elementary school, we had some English lessons. Our teacher wore a frock coat, and he used to take cards out his pocket with A, B, C written on them and teach us. I still remember how he looked. . . .

Sensei's bedroom was on the second floor, and below that was our classroom, and while I was there, I think there were two more rooms—an eight-mat tatami room and a six-mat room. . . .

It was a very old house that used to belong to a nobleman. Sensei let me sleep upstairs. It was a four-and-a-half-mat room and I slept there alone. Sensei was next door, in her bedroom. It was so old-fashioned, you probably can't imagine it—there were narrow stairs like a ladder and it was all very simple. Sensei and I slept and ate in the house together. The kitchen was so different (from American kitchens). In Japan, there was no gas—only coals—we cooked on a coal fire.

I didn't have trouble supporting myself. Because I was in Sensei's house. We sometimes had Western-style food, like roast chicken. That was a treat.

(Responding to a question about tuition)

It was very cheap. How much? I don't know. I think my husband paid. I don't know. I don't remember anything about money. . . .

Sensei usually wore a kimono. She wore a *hakama*[17] over that, and wore a watch here (on her breast), and she had a habit of fingering the chain. She was small, and short. Smaller than me. She had dimples on her hands—cute dimples. But she had short fingers. Because she was small. She put on weight easily. She was short, so (of course) she looked plump.

She sometimes put on old-fashioned Western-style dresses for ceremonies. From when she went to America a long time ago.

Sensei was frugal. She didn't like extravagance. It's funny that she remembered the Japanese way (of valuing frugality) when she went away so young.

. . . In the morning, she got up earlier than the students, then came her toilette, Japanese-style, and then breakfast with the students. After breakfast, she went directly to the school.

---

17 An article of traditional Japanese clothing, shaped like a long pleated skirt. It is tied at the waist and worn over a kimono. Originally worn mostly by men, *hakama* became popular among women students at the end of the Meiji period, because they permitted women more physical freedom and also protected delicate silk kimonos from wear and tear. *Hakama* are still worn by many women on special occasions relating to education, such as graduation ceremonies.

Sensei wasn't flexible—she was very strict about mistakes. No meant no. Even for a single word of English. "No, not yet, once more please," she would say. She was a very good teacher.

Sensei was so passionate about teaching. She had asthma, she was always wheezing and coughing—but even then, when she couldn't come to class, she would call students to her sickroom and teach them there. Japanese can't pronounce R and L properly. "Rrrr—top of your tongue up!" she would say. "Chin! Rrrr! Rrrr! Try again. No, not yet." That's how she was. She was strict. With her English (because it was perfect), wherever I went (in America), people would tell me "Good English!"

. . . You know, I became a Christian after I went to Tsuda. I was drawn to her, and she was a passionate Christian. To tell the truth, so many of the Americans I met over here acted in a way that wasn't Christian, so I was disappointed. I've forgotten about Christianity now.

. . . Sensei spoke English, but she used to practice Japanese writing by tracing lines in the ashes with those metal chopsticks we used to pick up coal. . . .

Sensei loved America . . . but she told us to keep the things that were deep in our hearts . . . the Japanese spirit . . . she said not to forget that we were Japanese. Speaking English is nothing, she said. Don't forget your Japanese spirit. That was the wonderful thing about Sensei. Yes, it really was. She really drummed that into our heads.

. . . She had Japanese discipline, the spirit, in her head. She went to America when she was seven and forgot all about Japan, but she came back to Japan after ten years, but it was in her head that she had to do something for Japan.

Every Saturday, she had dinner with the dormitory students, and after dinner, she told us about America and taught us so much. Things that would be useful to us as students. (Okamoto does not appear to remember details about the teachings, however.) Saturday night, she wrote letters. Every Saturday night, she never failed to write to Mrs. Lanman, who took care of her when she studied in America. It was my job to mail them for her. I went with two friends. Japanese mailboxes (in those days) they were like the trash bins here (in the nursing home). They were boxes with wooden lids that dropped shut after you put the letter in. They were old-fashioned. I put the letters in there. I think it took more than two weeks for them to cross the Pacific Ocean. So Sensei wrote a letter every Saturday night. She was different. She was mystifying, and admirable.

Sensei's room was stacked with books. She told me to use it like a library, and she let me borrow them—only me. I was very grateful.

. . . Sensei used to teach at the Peeresses' School, but it wasn't interesting for her. The level of Japanese women (the level of their education) was so low, she felt she had to raise it up a little. . . .

Sensei was humorous and she had a good, loud voice. She would laugh really loud—Ha! Ha! Ha! And she had the idea that she had to practice Japanese as much as possible, on her own.

She always had dinner with the students on Saturday, and after dinner, she told us stories, and she always spoke English. But after that, she switched to Japanese and we would have tea, and she would laugh—Ha! Ha! Ha! . . .

(Asked why she thought Tsuda-sensei remained single all her life.)

Well, she didn't say herself, and it was just guesswork on our part, but there was a scholar named Nakamura Kenzō. He was studying in America, and she liked him very much—that was the rumor. We picked up on things like that really fast (laughs), I don't know if it was true or not. Maybe she smiled a little bit (when we talked about it) . . . .

Okamura's story brings Umeko wonderfully to life. It also reveals how Japanese people lived in those days, which is why I have taken the liberty of presenting such a long excerpt.

The school building, when there were only ten students, was even smaller than the old nobleman's house in Okamura's story. It was an ordinary Japanese house with floor space of approximately 270 square meters. Two six-mat tatami rooms were used as classrooms, and one of them doubled as a dining room. The other doubled as Alice Bacon's bedroom-sitting room.

As evident from Okamura's story, Umeko believed that education was born of true contact between people, and those she educated in this way mostly loved and remembered her warmly for the rest of their lives. As noted by Okamura, the fledgling school accepted students like her who had finished only elementary school. It adapted itself to the academic needs of each student and did not discriminate against a woman because she was married. In fact, Umeko personally interviewed Okamura's husband and spoke with him at length.

When I was at Tsuda College from 1949 to 1953, some students entered the school after marrying and some married while they were there, which was rare at other colleges. It reflected Umeko's unfettered and natural attitude toward the different ways that people live their lives. Umeko remained single all her life, but she made no distinction between people who married and those who did not. She gave opportunities to all who wanted to learn.

Okamura Shina went to America in 1907, three years after her husband. Umeko and Anna Hartshorne arranged for her to accompany a government mission that traveled at the same time. In later years, Okamura visited Umeko whenever she returned to Japan to see her family.

After taping the interviews, Murakami related the dramatic story of Okamura Shina and the people in her life in a book titled *Hyakunen*

no yume (A Century of Dreams), which was published by Shinchōsha.[18]
Hyakunen no yume is not Umeko's story, but it is a valuable record of a
hundred years in the history of Japan and America that more or less coin-
cides with Umeko's lifetime. Okamura Shinako passed away in 1984 at the
age of 102.

18 Murakami Yumiko, *Hyakunen no yume* [A Century of Dreams] (Tokyo: Shinchōsha, 1989).

CHAPTER

10

SEEDLINGS

Umeko went to America when she was seven years old and was eighteen when she returned to Japan after eleven years of study. Okamura Shinako was born that same year, in 1882. She grew up and studied at Joshi Eigaku Juku, the school that Umeko founded. Shinako later lived for many years in the United States and passed away at the age of 102.

Umeko died in 1929 and I was born a year later, in 1930. From early childhood to adolescence, I grew up in the middle of a long war. From 1949 to 1953, between the ages of eighteen and twenty-two, I was a student at Tsuda College in the town of Kodaira. This is the link that led me to write this book.

It was shortly after the Pacific War and the Japanese people were still hungry and desperately poor in the material sense. But spiritually, my four years in the college dormitory that stood in the Musashino woods of the western Kantō plain were the richest of my life. The students were young and full of rebellious thoughts, each in our own individual way, but we shared an odd devotion to Tsuda Umeko, the founder of our school.

A portrait of Umeko hung in the college auditorium, showing her in a drab kimono, sitting comfortably in a chair, looking like a humble farmer's wife. There was nothing stylish about her. *Après guerre* was a term often heard in those days, referring to the postwar youth, aimless and adrift. Indeed, plenty of students strode about campus in bright, flashy clothing and behaved accordingly, but even they were conscious of Umeko looking out at them from her portrait.

We students were aware that however we chose to live our lives, we had the power of people like Umeko behind us, and our teachers had an eye on everything we said and did. Each of us had to pledge to maintain pride and honor by being responsible for every word and action—that was the school tradition. Unlike many Japanese schools of the day, there was no whiff of totalitarianism on our campus. Individuality was respected, but we were also rigorously judged by what we achieved.

During the first year at college, we were expected to take stock of our academic ability. Those unable to keep up with the teaching methods were welcome to go elsewhere, and there was a general feeling that they would not be regretted if they did. Skipping class was nearly impossible, and anyone who did so repeatedly almost certainly failed the course. There were not many students back then, and most of the classes were conducted like seminars, in groups of twenty or fewer. If we missed a class, it was difficult to keep up with the next one. Homework was checked with great severity, and we could not earn credits unless every assignment and every test received a passing grade. The idea was that a lazy student was wasting her tuition.

I was blessed with generous friends who helped me with my homework, so I somehow managed to graduate, although on barely passing grades. It puzzled me for a long time as to how I could have been lucky enough to have such friends in a school that focused so much on individual achievement. But now, thinking back, I am not as puzzled as I used to be. I was completely absorbed in reading literature—which did not interest most of the others—and I was distracted from studying English because I was too busy writing dense, half-baked novels. My friends helped me, I think, because they decided that literature must be my special gift. They had somehow absorbed the idea handed down from Umeko that individuality and each individual must be respected. In any case, it was thanks to my friends that I was able to earn a bachelor's degree at Tsuda College, and it is a diploma that has served me well throughout my life.

In most of the countries I have visited, I usually found a Tsuda graduate or two in the capital and in almost every college town. Whenever I traveled and came to a city for the first time, one of them would treat me with great kindness simply because I was a fellow graduate. Tsuda was a small school, so we usually knew each other by sight if we were students within three or four years of each other, and if the age gap was greater, common memories of classrooms and teachers brought us together and quickly made us feel like old friends. It was not my being a writer that made these connections possible. Even when I was quite young and completely unknown, fellow alumnae were incredibly kind to me and treated me like a friend with whom they had shared their lives until just the other day.

There was a general feeling on campus that personal relationships are to be valued, because bonds formed in that way are a joyful part of being alive. Ever since Umeko founded the school, students were one family, unrelated by blood but united by having learned together. The year I entered the school, I think there was at least one student from every prefecture in Japan. Most of them had chosen the school through the influence of someone who had been influenced by Umeko or one of her students.

Just now, I am about to have some tea, accompanied by a sweet called "Lingering Snow on Mount Chōkai." The sweets evoke a landscape of lingering snow on purple mountaintops, and they were sent to me by Kawaguchi Eiko, who lives in the city of Akita. Kawaguchi studied at Tsuda shortly after the Great Kantō Earthquake, and before that, she was a classmate of my mother at a girls' high school.

My mother was not a Tsuda graduate, but no doubt heard about the school from Kawaguchi. And my grandfather, who was born in the Ansei era (1854–1860), often mentioned Tsuda Sen and his novel agricultural methods, so the name of the school and its founder were familiar to me. This may have influenced my choice of this school for college.

The intimate web of personal relationships that encircled the small private school could be irksome, but there was always a sense of living, breathing, individual human beings—something that larger schools lacked. There was an atmosphere of trust between people who abided by the Tsuda creed of looking squarely at an individual and making one's own judgments.

I sensed the same atmosphere at Umeko's alma mater, Bryn Mawr College. Whenever I met graduates of that school during my time in America, I was able to gain a certain level of trust because Tsuda Umeko, who had studied at Bryn Mawr and then established a school, was also Japanese, and because I was a graduate of that school.

The credits I earned at Tsuda were rated highly, at least in the U.S., enabling me to enroll at American colleges on favorable terms, and even helped me to gain employment (as a part-time teacher) at a time when such things were difficult for residents with Japanese citizenship.

A fair number of the Tsuda graduates I met in various countries had put down roots in foreign lands. Some had foreign spouses, and others had stayed on to teach at foreign universities because Japanese society rarely allowed women of our generation to work in positions that matched their ability.

Ikawa Fumiko, a professor of archaeology at McGill University in Montreal, Canada, and Kishimoto Haruko, a geographer at the University of Zurich in Switzerland, were both classmates of mine and are good examples of brain drain from Japan. They were both hospitable when I dropped by and invited me to stay in their homes.

Four other Tsuda graduates, Yamakawa Kikue, Fujita Taki, Moriyama Mayumi, and Akamatsu Ryōko, are among the postwar directors of the Women's and Minors' Bureau of Japan's labor ministry. Each opened new paths to women during their tenure, before passing the torch to their successors.

Anthropologist Nakane Chie, former chief cabinet secretary Moriyama Mayumi, and Akamatsu Ryōko—who was also active in the diplomatic sphere—all studied at Tsuda (a vocational school during their enrollment) before going on to the University of Tokyo, which opened its doors to women for the first time after the war. The three women succeeded in passing the rigorous entrance examination alongside young men from Japan's most elite boys' high schools. It was during Akamatsu Ryōko's tenure as director of the Women's Bureau that the groundbreaking law for women—the Equal Employment Opportunity Act—was enacted.

Each of these Tsuda graduates inherited and promoted the founder's intention of leading women into a place in the sun. The women whose names I mention here were, in a manner of speaking, women in the limelight of the Shōwa era. But there were countless other graduates, unnamed, who bloomed quietly on branches that grew from seeds planted by Tsuda Umeko, and in their turn scattered new seeds. Just like the frogs' eggs that divided and multiplied under Umeko's microscope a hundred years ago.

Today, in the 1990s, when most Japanese colleges and universities are coeducational, Tsuda College remains an institution for women. Many of America's distinguished women's colleges have also become coeducational, but Bryn Mawr remains a women's college. Credits may be exchanged with other institutions and there is a great deal of interaction with men at other colleges, but I have come to believe that there is a reason for the existence of women's colleges.

People of my generation spent much of their young childhood and adolescence in a long-drawn-out war, and the school system was switched from the old system to a new one in the middle of our education. I began college just as the new system came into being, but did not attend a coeducational school until after I had finished college. But such schools were coming into existence, and as a young woman, I was somewhat envious of people who went to school with members of the opposite sex.

Later, I went to the U.S. and experienced coeducation at American universities, and still later, taught at a coeducational university (in Japan) where I had a chance to mingle with students on campus. These experiences led me think that it may be a good idea to spend at least a few years of one's life in a boys' or girls' school.

Why? Taking girls as an example, at a women's university or a girls' high school, when students undertake a project or study assignment and no one of the opposite sex is available, the girls do everything for themselves, including tasks that are normally allotted to boys. In situations like this, they have a chance to devise their own way of doing things. This can be an opportunity to discover unexpected abilities within themselves.

For example, when I was at college, I was more or less in charge of a theatrical group and found myself managing and organizing everything, from acting and directing to things like carpentry, lighting, and costumes. If ours had been a coeducational school, a spontaneous division of roles would have occurred, with girls taking on the women's roles and being in charge of costumes and such. This manner of doing things leads to discrimination on the basis of preconceived gender roles and the effect is to suppress the dormant abilities or talents a person might have. This holds not only for girls but for boys as well. Men are deprived of the chance to develop abilities that they may actually possess, but which are normally thought of as being feminine, simply because the women around them are too willing to do those tasks for them.

Women who have attended women's colleges often voice the following complaint about women graduates of coeducational schools: "They defer so much to men and don't speak their own minds!" On a women-only campus, women say what they mean because they mean it—which can lead to some very heated arguments, whereas women on coeducational campuses stand by and let the men do the arguing, they say.

Experiences in later life have made me think that this is a real tendency. It is natural to spend most of one's life in contact with members of the opposite sex; since men and women each make up roughly half of humanity, it goes without saying that the distinctive traits of the other half should be respected. However, it is by no means a waste of time to spend a few years of the many decades of one's life exclusively in the company of one's own sex. The unnaturalness and inconvenience of the situation makes you yearn for the abilities of the other half, and makes you realize that it is better to have people of both sexes around to lean on. That in itself is an important discovery. For these reasons, I personally hope that my alma mater will go on being a women's school.

In December 1989, Maejima Shūji, a teacher at Seian Girls' High School in Kyoto, sent the editorial department of *Gekkan Asahi* forty-eight essays written by first-year students of the school after reading the first few chapters of *Tsuda Umeko* (which was originally published as a serial in the monthly magazine). Nothing makes a writer happier than favorable responses from readers. I read all the essays with great interest and was deeply touched that these young people, born more than a century after Umeko, could feel such empathy for her. Below are some excerpts from the essays:

> When our teacher handed out the first part of *Tsuda Umeko* in our civics class, my first thought was: "No way I'm going to read such a long text." But then I heard that we would have to write something about it in our mid-terms, so I started on it, unwillingly. But once I began, I got interested in Umeko and kept reading and reading. Maybe I'm exaggerating, but reading the *Umeko* series really changed my life. Back then, when men were all powerful, she raised women up. They used to think that women belonged to men, but Umeko broke through the stereotype.
>
> Umeko had a magnetic personality. Everybody recognized her worth. I don't think she could have attracted so many people just by being a good scholar. She had everything—intelligence and warmth—and a sense of humor.
>
> . . . Her spirited behavior . . . and the wonderful way she lived her life attracted people to her and made them support her, and everyone around her sort of caught the Umeko bug. I'm one of the people she infected. . . . (Student A)

. . . Tsuda Umeko was attracted to men, and she was a woman who appreciated masculine strength. I think this is very natural. . . . The fact that we help each other means that people can't do things all by themselves. (Student B)

I think Tsuda Umeko was a person who considered the discrimination of women from the viewpoint of economic independence. So she studied and she thought. Then she went to America to study, but I wonder what it was that America had back then. What was it about America that made it a place of dreams and hope for Japan? What was the difference between America and Japan? . . . With regard to gender discrimination, I think that's one aspect where America is freer than Japan. . . . I attend a private school, and I wonder why . . . I had doubts (about lots of things) that made me go to Seian Girls' School instead of a public school. People in my neighborhood all think public schools are best, but I don't agree. . . . I read *Tsuda Umeko* today and learned about Tsuda Umeko's life and the way she thought. I learned about women's lives, position, and education, and about her private school. Then I thought about how I should live my own life. . . . I decided that I'm glad I go to a private school. (Student C)

The essays were class assignments, so no doubt there is an element of trying to please the teacher. Nevertheless, I think they are alive with the minds of young people responding to Umeko's passion. I ended Chapter 8 of this book with Carey Thomas's words: "Believe in woman." The words must have left an impression on the girls, because quite a few of them wrote that they agreed. I have quoted portions of their essays because I wanted to share their reaction with my readers, together with expressing gratitude to their teacher, Mr. Maejima.

I have repeatedly noted Umeko's ability to charm. She had opportunities to meet various distinguished people in her lifetime, and she invariably left an impression. When she attended the 1898 International Women's Federation Meeting in Denver as the Japanese delegate, several eminent English ladies invited her to visit their country, and she stayed in Europe for half a year.

During her visit to England she met the Archbishop of York and his wife, and there, she arrived at a personal understanding of life as a Christian. At their meeting, the archbishop told Umeko that he had preached doctrine in his younger years, but as he grew older, he began to think only about the love and life of Christ, and he now believed that it was not good works or doctrines that mattered, but only how much one was like Him. Then he wrote out for her a verse from the Bible: "Grow in the grace and knowledge of our Lord and Saviour Jesus Christ" (2 Peter 3:18).[1]

Umeko did not speak or preach about Christianity in public, but her faith is evident in many of her letters to Adeline. For example, she remarks that many Japanese are unduly devastated and grieved by the deaths of loved ones because they do not believe in life after death. In fact, Umeko did not break down when she lost her parents and very close friends. She quietly watched their passing and had faith in their resurrection.

She poured every bit of her body and soul into her school and gave it all her vitality. In this sense, her students were her life after death, and there was no need for her to proselytize. I remember that we were given the opportunity to study the Bible as literature, and that church services and Bible study classes took place somewhere on campus, but that was all. This was the spirit of freedom that the Lanmans had instilled in her as a young child, and it was the kind of faith she confirmed through her meeting with the Archbishop of York.

---

1   *Tsuda Umeko bunsho*, 295.

Umeko also met Florence Nightingale, eighty years old at the time, during her stay in England. She describes her impressions of the encounter and their exchange of views about the future in the March 20, 1899 entry of her London diary. The detailed narrative reads like a scene out of a film.[2]

The *Tsuda Umeko bunsho* also includes an account of her meeting with Helen Keller. This was based on an oral account given by Umeko in Japanese, and published as a series of three articles in *Jogaku kōgi* (Lectures for Women) between February and April 1901. Umeko's visit with Helen took place in August 1898 and was probably an opportunity that emerged through her participation in the Denver conference.

I was greatly drawn to Umeko's narrative of her meeting with Helen Keller, the accomplished deaf and blind girl who was very much in the news around that time. Umeko remarks on Helen's remarkable literary talent and her knack for putting words together, and suggests that this was due to her way of seeing things with the eyes of her soul. She describes how the deaf and blind girl understood objects and ideas by linking to them to signs, and she explains in detail how Miss Sullivan, the woman who taught Helen, brought this about.

> At this time there was a doll that Helen was very fond of, which she always kept by her side, and this became the first tool with which Miss Sullivan taught her. To teach her that things have a name and that there is a sign that expresses that name, and to teach her which sign signifies a certain thing, she formed the sign for "doll" in Helen's hand with her fingertips and did the same thing day after day for three months, until Helen finally understood the connection. That is, until she began to understand that when Miss Sullivan touched her palm with her fingers and moved them in a certain way, she meant

---

2 Ibid., 335–38.

the doll. This opened the way to teaching her other things, and she taught her many names by the same process, so that after about five months, Helen knew 625 signs. She could also make the signs herself and read books in Braille. . . .

Helen also showed me how she studied geometry. She had a number of sturdy sticks with wires attached to them so that she could connect them to form triangles and squares, in order for her to think about them theoretically. . . .

Helen was very innocent, and not at all worldly. She was sweet and almost childlike. She was world famous and people spoke of her as an extraordinary and enigmatic girl, but Helen never heard this and was unconcerned. . . .[3]

Helen became deaf and blind when she was very young and had the temperament of a wild, unmanageable animal, but when education gave her the ability to express herself, she turned into a completely mild-mannered person. When Umeko saw the girl before her—deaf and blind but able to clearly see the beauty of the universe with the eyes and ears of her mind, and possessed of an abundant faculty for self-expression—she must have thought about what it was to teach Japanese girls a foreign language. In teaching them the speech of a foreign land, she was bringing them into contact with the impulses of the soul that lie hidden in the depths of that language.

It is said that Umeko's Japanese remained somewhat stilted and foreign until the end of her life, but I suspect that this was so because she was so incredibly sensitive to language that she was incapable of merely parroting the things she heard or read. Umeko translated many classical Japanese works of literature into English and she was also a great reader of

---

3   Ibid., 29–40.

contemporary literature, both Japanese and English. She had a fine literary sensibility and an extraordinary attachment to language.

Umeko met many people in many fields, both famous and unknown. She enjoyed listening to them and was naively curious and respectful toward all, without regard for status. Her girlish attitude was accompanied by a complete self-assurance that enabled her to speak her mind clearly when necessary, and to listen to people with complete absorption and seriousness when called for. The gentility and sincerity of her curiosity are what made people open their hearts to her, and why every encounter gave pleasure that left a lasting impression.[4]

Ever since the founding of her school, Umeko's days and nights had been filled with its management and with planning for the futures of her young students (which included sending them abroad for further study). Her letters to Adeline were full of repetitions of how busy she was, and offered little of the colorful, lively descriptiveness of twenty years earlier, when she was fresh off the boat from America and surprised or shocked at everything she saw in the country of her birth. Adeline was also older and growing absent-minded, and Umeko's letters tended toward soothing responses to her complaints or gossip about old acquaintances.

Among such letters are a few that shine like a ripple of sunlight on a somber sea. These are the ones written while she was traveling. Umeko loved to travel, and although inspection tours and such were often gruelingly hectic, now and then she had a chance to relax.

In 1907, Umeko, accompanied by her younger sister Yonako, traveled to Italy (via America). On December 12, they sailed from Naples to Capri.

---

4   Umeko also met with President and Mrs. Roosevelt in 1907, to whom she told the story of the forty-seven loyal retainers. This is a famous story about forty-seven samurai of the early eighteenth century who dramatically avenged the death of their lord. Called *Chūshingura*, it is often performed in kabuki and bunraku.

. . . Yona says I have grown fat and indeed I am very well and resting nicely since I came over to Italy. Roses and narcissuses are blooming and oranges and lemons are on all the trees. It agrees with me finely, and I only wish I could stay here a month or two, and take in the wine of this fine air.

S.S. *Prinz Heinrich*
in the Red Sea
December 26, 1907

. . . The sea has not been very rough, fortunately, and so Yona and I are keeping up very well indeed. I take a sea bath in the big bath tub nearly every day, and the rest of the time lie in my steamer chair, very, very lazy indeed—don't do much reading or writing either. I ought to do some work, but I am entirely too lazy to do anything at all. Well, perhaps the perfect rest is good for me. . . .

Despite these words, Umeko was meeting old acquaintances in every country she visited, and through them making new friends. Umeko's reputation passed by word of mouth from person to person, and at least in social circles of the American East, she seems to have been held in high regard. The Philadelphia committee surrounding Mrs. Morris was supporting the growth of Joshi Eigaku Juku and still collecting large donations. Mr. and Mrs. Henry Woods, philanthropists from Boston, donated enough funds to build the Henry Woods Hall, which was large enough to seat four hundred people. One letter to Adeline mentions a visitor from Chicago who donated five hundred dollars to Joshi Eigaku Juku. Five hundred dollars was a substantial amount for an individual donation in those days.

America had become a great manufacturing nation ahead of Japan, with the world's wealth in its pockets. Affluent citizens of the American East were contributing a portion of that wealth to enable the women of Asia to enjoy a better future. A century later, Japan is collecting the world's wealth in a similar way, and perhaps there are Japanese somewhere, helping someone—an African Umeko or Southeast Asian Umeko—to achieve their dream. Wealth accumulated in one place passed along to where it can give birth to a new force—that is life functioning the way it is supposed to do.

Umeko enjoyed being surrounded by her many students, but she was so busy. It was only when she traveled that she could find time for herself and feel a modicum of relief. When she crossed borders and spoke with people in foreign lands, her eyes regained the brightness and alertness of the eighteen-year-old girl who returned to Japan. The great sense of duty that overwhelmed her in 1882, the young passion that told her that her mission was to build a future for Japanese women—this is what energized her throughout her life.

People interested Umeko more than anything and up to her very last years, hardly a day went by that she did not have visitors. Her letters to Adeline indicate that she daily met with several people, sometimes as many as ten, and this was in addition to the students she taught.

Adeline Lanman, who by this time is probably as familiar as an old friend to readers of this book, passed away in 1914 at the age of eighty-eight, when Umeko was fifty years old. Charles Lanman had passed away in 1895, Umeko's father Sen in 1908, and her mother Hatsuko died the following year. Umeko had lost both her natural and foster parents, but she still had the school that was her life, and the students the school had nurtured.

The correspondence with Adeline—the long letters that Umeko wrote like a diary and posted over many decades—also came to an end. Umeko kept a diary throughout her life in addition to these letters, but few of the diaries have survived. However, the correspondence cited in this book can be read as a diary, and also as a spiritual chronicle of a woman of that time and age.

Umeko began to suffer from diabetes and high blood pressure around 1917, and subsequently had a series of strokes that required hospitalization. She was bedridden for the last decade of her life, and although she might take a walk on good days with some assistance, there was no question of her resuming her duties at the school. She appears to have spent the decade of retirement in tranquility—the first such period in her life—reliving old memories and dreaming of the future.

Alice Bacon passed away in 1918 and Ōyama Sutematsu in 1919. They were her comrades-in-arms—the people who shared her life abroad and in Japan, who lived as women of the same era and dreamed of a better future for other women, and who stood by Umeko and her school. Their dream was becoming a reality, and Umeko was surrounded by young seedlings on their way to maturity.

The land for the present-day campus of Tsuda University in Kodaira was acquired in 1922. However, the following year, 1923, was the year of the Great Kantō Earthquake and the Gobanchō school burned to the ground in the ensuing fires. Umeko heard the news in her sickbed, but it was reported that she remained calm. She held to her faith that visible and material things may be consumed by fire, but what is nurtured within living human beings cannot be lost. After all, she had said in her opening address of Joshi Eigaku Juku that education was not achieved by fine buildings, but through the give and take between teachers and students.

Anna Hartshorne, Umeko's remaining longtime collaborator, left for America to raise funds to rebuild the devastated school. Anna Hartshorne was sixty-three years old, but she took over Umeko's role and based herself in New York to appeal for donations. She collected 500,000 yen in three years and returned to Japan. Donations kept coming in, and when the sum reached 1.3 million yen in 1928, concrete plans for the new Kodaira campus began to take shape. Umeko watched quietly from afar and spent her days peacefully in the company of her trusted successors. A steady stream of old students came to call on her. I wonder what she thought of them.

Umeko lived her final years as an invalid, reading and knitting and sending knitted articles to her friends and close acquaintances. It may seem odd to think that this woman of unbelievable energy, a woman who was always up and about and on the move, could sit quietly in a cane chair and knit. But for some reason, the image of Umeko knitting seems very real to me—actually, more real than real. Nothing would have suited her better.

Knitting is often regarded as meaningless busywork for elderly women, but I have recently discovered, through experience, that keeping the fingers in motion improves circulation throughout the whole body; the benefit is similar to that of walking. Umeko must have knitted and gone back and forth in her mind between past and future, enjoying little discoveries along the way, similar to a philosopher or mathematician unexpectedly encountering new ideas in the course of a walk. I used to scorn this painstaking craft that advances stitch by patient stitch, but I was foolish. I did not realize that knitting is akin to thinking while walking.

With regard to knitting, when Umeko first returned to Japan, she often asked Adeline to send yarn and knitting needles so that she could knit afghans, which were almost unknown in Japan at the time, for her aunts, friends, and acquaintances. She must have had the old knitting patterns in her memory, and looked back on her life as she worked the needles.

After Sutematsu, her old friend Uriu (Nagai) Shigeko also passed away. On the evening of August 16, 1929, Umeko suffered a hemorrhagic stroke and quietly breathed her last. Her diary entry for that day was just three words.

Fri.—16. Storm last night.

They are poignant words. Yamazaki Takako begins her biography, *Tsuda Umeko*, with these words. Umeko's bedside diary of short phrases ends abruptly, like a quietly played violin string silenced in mid-melody. It is an ending that makes you think about life and infinity. Umeko was sixty-four years and eight months old.

Two biographies of Tsuda Umeko have been published (in Japan): Yoshikawa Toshikazu's *Tsuda Umeko den* and Yamazaki Takako's *Tsuda Umeko*. Both authors were at Tsuda during my student years and were known to me personally. Yoshikawa worked as an administrator for thirty-six years and visited Umeko's bedside every week during her last years while writing *Tsuda Umeko*, a book that was published in 1930 by Fujo Shimbunsha. (The book's revised edition was later republished in 1956 as *Tsuda Umeko den* by the Tsuda Juku Dōsōkai [Tsuda Alumnae Association].) The book appeared after her death, but Umeko read it in manuscript form. Yoshikawa's biography is replete with admiration, bordering on adoration, as if he were overwhelmed by her very presence. Much of the book is based on Umeko's own words, giving it an autobiographical bent.

Yamazaki Takako taught Japanese language and literature while I was at college. She had studied at Tsuda and then studied Japanese literature at Kyushu University. Her *Tsuda Umeko* appeared as part of Yoshikawa Kōbunkan's Library of Biographies series. It was published in 1962 and has been reprinted many times.

Yamazaki was editor in chief of *Tsuda Juku Rokujunen-shi* (A Sixty-Year History of Tsuda School), which was published by the college in 1960. Though she was a Tsuda graduate and taught at the school, she took a more detached view of Umeko in her biography than Yoshikawa and depicted her in a different way. Yamazaki was an ardent Christian who delved deeply into Umeko's Christianity in a manner I found very satisfying. In her preface, she commemorates Umeko with words from the Bible: "And whosoever will lose his life for my sake shall find it" (Matthew 16:25).

I described in an earlier chapter how I came to write this particular book about Tsuda Umeko. In 1984, several hundred letters written by

Umeko over a period of thirty years to her foster mother in America, Adeline Lanman, were found in an attic room of Tsuda College. They were personal letters, written by Umeko from the time she was eighteen until she was middle-aged, and I thought they might form the basis of a different image of Umeko, not as a public historical figure, but as a living, breathing woman, and that I could convey that living image to contemporary readers.

That was my purpose, and the result is far from an academic study of Tsuda Umeko. I want the reader to understand it as an effort by the writer Ōba Minako to recreate an image of Umeko as part of her study of human nature. Aside from Umeko's own letters, most of the reference material and sources are mentioned only in passing. My focus has always been on conveying the charm of Umeko's writing style and of the person who emerges from her words. As a former student of her school and one of a long line of torchbearers, I hope this book will help to revive the figure of a woman who dreamt of a better life for women and became a pioneer in the time of our mothers and grandmothers.

My book *Tsuda Umeko* debuted as a serial in the inaugural issue of the monthly magazine *Gekkan Asahi*. The editor was Ōue Asami, who helped me with research, reviewed my manuscripts with great care, and always encouraged me with well-chosen words of advice and criticism. I also extend my sincere thanks to Sumikura Jirō, editor in chief, and Shigekane Atsuyuki, sub editor in chief of the magazine. Mitsui Eiichi's artwork enhanced the series with historically accurate illustrations and brought to life the visual trappings of Umeko's life. Together with anecdotes from people who had known her, the illustrations were a great help in imagining how things must have been.

I cannot begin to imagine the labor involved in sorting, deciphering, and transcribing by typewriter and word processor the mountain of letters handwritten by Umeko over thirty years. It was a group of people at Tsuda College who undertook this tremendous task. My husband Toshio helped me to wade through the voluminous transcripts, which we somehow got through with many a squabble along the way.

Consider the amount of work by a great many people, brought together through a long chain of circumstances, that is required for one, small book like this to be produced. Then imagine the multitudes and the amassed power that must gone into helping Tsuda Umeko to realize her vision.

At the moment, I am feeling as if I have lived alongside Umeko for several decades. I am roughly the same age as she was toward the end, and am feeling likewise very tired and suffering from some of the same ailments. It seems a good time to set my brush and ink aside. When I look up, there are new buds on the branches of the plum tree outside my window.

When Umeko was born, her father Sen was so disappointed that she was not a boy that he stormed out of the house in a rage and did not come home that night. The baby had no name after seven days, so her mother Hatsuko contemplated the bonsai plum tree near her pillow, and seeing that a flower was about to bloom, she named the child Ume (plum blossom).

An orchard of plum trees was planted on the Kodaira campus in memory of Umeko. The buds were usually swelling when students returned to the dormitories after the New Year's holiday. I remember seeing droplets of light on dew-moistened plum petals as my classmates and I wandered under the trees and talked about our futures in the cold moonlight of early spring nights.

Only a few pages are left for me to write, and I would like to finish with some anecdotes told to us when we were students—anecdotes about the school in wartime. When I began college, Hoshino Ai was president of the school. Hoshino was a member of the fourth graduating class and had been tutored personally by Umeko. She had been at Joshi Eigaku Juku, then Tsuda Eigaku Juku, then Tsuda Juku Vocational College, and finally Tsuda College, and she had overseen the move to Kodaira and added a science department to the school.

After finishing her studies at Joshi Eigaku Juku, Hoshino went to Bryn Mawr to study biology and chemistry. She performed so well on her mathematics test for the entrance examination that the school recommended that she major in mathematics. I think it was her scientific and level-headed thinking that made it possible to overcome the many difficulties encountered by the school toward the end of the war and after it was over. The science department, established in 1943, eventually became the department of mathematics.

The history of this department is presented in a book called *Josei no jiritsu to kagaku kyōiku* (Independence for Women and Science Education), which was published in 1987. The first graduating class of the science department had gathered ten years earlier to celebrate the thirtieth anniversary of their graduation, and they decided to put together a record of the difficult years of their youth, which were also tempestuous years for the college. One of the episodes related in the book is as follows:

As anyone who was of school age or older will surely remember, in those days, every school in Japan displayed a photograph of the emperor and empress. It might be in the office of the principal, or sometimes there was a special building for that purpose. Students were not permitted to pass before them without bowing.

However, there was no portrait anywhere on the Tsuda campus.

Fujita Taki, who was President Hoshino Ai's assistant and always at her side, recalls what happened.

During the war, the ministry of education repeatedly reminded the school of its duty to display the portraits. "Such portraits must not be treated frivolously. We have no suitable place to display them" was the answer given by President Hoshino. An official came to check and ordered that they be placed in the president's office. "There are classrooms above the office. Students would walk over the portraits, and we could not possibly condone such a great irreverence." The exasperated official ordered her to build a shrine somewhere on the school premises and went away, but Japan soon lost the war and nothing more came of the plan.[5]

Another episode is related in Hoshino Ai's *Shōden: Denki* (Recollections):

It was March 1944 when we took on factory work at the school....We wanted to keep our students as safe as possible, and if feasible, to enable them to study between work shifts, so having a factory on the school grounds seemed to be the best solution. The work was very light at first, but the Americans began to bomb the mainland in the autumn, and large factories began to evacuate their machinery. Our women students were soon working at lathes like men, in three shifts that continued through the night....

We faced a new problem in early May, when the army moved into our school buildings. They took over one dormitory and most of the lecture halls, so we were squeezed into the east dormitory and office, faculty rooms, and the president's office. All of the boarding students were moved into one dormitory, which became overcrowded, while all the classrooms were used by the military. Even then, in between factory work, we managed to conduct some classes in the plum orchard and in the faculty building. The plaque incident occurred shortly after the army moved in.

The so-called plaque incident happened in this way: the army put up a plaque on the main gatepost to indicate its presence, and some

5   *Josei no jiritsu to kagaku kyōiku* [Independence for Women and Science Education], ed. Tsuda Juku Rika no Rekishi o Kirokusuru Kai [Tsuda Juku Committee for the Documentation of Science Education] (Tokyo: Domesu Shuppan, 1987), 156–57.

students sneaked out at night, removed it, and threw it into the river. The gatepost on the right originally had a plaque with the school's name, but the army had taken it down and ostentatiously placed two military plaques, one on each gatepost, left and right. Four students who were very upset about the removal of the school name committed their act of sabotage. Needless to say, there was a great commotion the next morning. We took it as a silly prank, but the outrage of the military was so extreme that we realized that the situation was very, very serious. The army insisted that we investigate and ferret out the culprits. I called the students together, assured them that they would be protected and that I would take full responsibility, and I asked the guilty parties to make themselves known. The four were determined not to tell. The army said in that case they would investigate for themselves and even threatened a court martial. Several distressing days went by, but on the third day, the four came to me and confessed. They had agonized over this decision, but as the original act had been motivated by their loyalty to the school, they decided that it would be counterproductive if the school came to harm because of their deed. . . . I went to see the officers again and apologized very respectfully, explaining that the incident had occurred because the army placed a plaque on both sides of the gate, so perhaps they could remove one of them and permit the school plaque to remain. This was May 1945, when the Japanese army was clearly in retreat, so perhaps the men were less sure of themselves. The ranking officer understood my position quite well. The four students were required to write an apology, but addressed only to me, and I was not forced to hand over their names. I was really very worried for a while, but it ended much better than I had expected.

. . . August came and we began to hear rumors that the war would soon end. When Japan accepted the conditions of the Potsdam

Declaration on August 15, we all gathered in the dining hall of the east dormitory and listened to the emperor on the radio. Many of the students wept. The war had kept them from studying as they wished, so I told them that we would take three days off to recover from our fatigue, then we would throw ourselves into study. But the next day a summons came from Maeda, the minister of education. The American Occupation was about to begin and the girls would be safer at home with their families, so the school must be closed, and they did not know when it could open again. On the eighteenth, we called the students to the lecture hall, assured them that we would soon have them back again, conducted an end-of-term ceremony and closed the school. We reopened on October 1.

. . . American forces were stationed nearby and soldiers came to the campus nearly every day. They didn't do much harm, aside from sneaking a box or two from the president's office, and I saw bearded soldiers bathing in the stream that ran alongside the school, which I found unsettling. One day, as I was having lunch, Honma [the janitor] ran into the room and told me that American soldiers were on campus and loading things onto a truck. I rushed to the scene and found them in the gym, removing the basketball goals. In the truck were desks, chairs, medical equipment, and medical supplies. I approached the officer who seemed to be in charge and told him the history of the school, and that the students would soon be back and they would no doubt be very sad if there were no desks or chairs. He listened to me coolly, then turned to the men and said "Boys, I think you had better take them down." It wasn't an order, and he spoke very calmly. The soldiers reluctantly unloaded the truck and went away. The next day, an Off Limits sign was put up near the school gate and they never came on campus again. When I think back, I realize that the soldiers had probably been put into shabby quarters with no tables or chairs and they really wanted our equipment. I don't recall his name, but I think the officer was a high school art teacher.[6]

Hoshino Ai's *Shōden: Denki* takes up the history of the school after Umeko, and unfolds like a continuation of Umeko's own story. Several of Hoshino's poems appear at the end of the book, and I quote one of them in remembrance of this remarkable teacher, and in anticipation of those who will come after.

> I have no husband or child
> But nearby to give me joy
> Are the many whom I taught

---

6 Hoshino Ai. *Shōden: Denki* [Recollections] (Tokyo: Ōzorasha, 1990), 97–102.

Tsuda University today.
Photo courtesy of Tsuda University.

COMMENTARY

In 2000, ten years after *Tsuda Umeko* was first published, Tsuda University celebrated its 100th anniversary. To commemorate the event, the university's alumnae association created a documentary film entitled *Yume wa toki o koete: Tsuda Umeko ga tsumuida kizuna* (A Dream across Time and Place: The Legacy of Tsuda Umeko) written and directed by Fujiwara Tomoko (released in October 2000). The book was mentioned near the end of the film, followed by an interview with the author, Ōba Minako. Ōba had suffered a debilitating stroke four years earlier and was confined to a wheelchair, but she was neatly dressed in a kimono and spoke emotionally, sometimes verging on tears.

> There are graduates of our college in the United States—not only there, of course; all over the world—but when I was in the U.S. I met some of them and they helped me, I thought that going to a college like Tsuda had given me a huge advantage. And when I saw those letters, I realized that TSUDA Umeko had been a person with a talent for writing and I was tremendously impressed.
>
> We live by language, after all. And language lives long. And what she taught us with so much enthusiasm was the essence of language.

Deep inside, that which we call language is something like the life of people. If you think like that, she will be satisfied.[1]

In her book *Tsuda Umeko*, Ōba frequently uses the expression "what lies behind words" as she follows and describes Umeko's life, her thoughts, and her aspirations. She also looks back on her own years at Tsuda College from 1949 to 1953. More than 400 letters written by Umeko to her host parents in America were discovered in 1984, and Ōba translates and creatively ponders the letters, probing for "what lies within the writer's words." In doing so, she sheds light on the context behind the project that Tsuda Umeko threw herself into body and soul, which was the founding of Tsuda College, the precursor of Tsuda University.

In 1900, Tsuda Umeko established Tsuda College, "the first school in Japan to provide women with a specialized higher education," initially with just ten students. In an era when women could not enroll in colleges, this school began as a private institution of higher learning that offered women specialized courses in accordance with Umeko's educational ideals, which aspired to train women so they could become financially independent as teachers of English at secondary schools for girls.[2]

Graduates of the school include a long line of women pioneers. Ōba lists some of them in Chapter 10: several directors of the Women's and Minors' Bureau of the Ministry of Labor, beginning with Yamakawa Kikue, followed by Fujita Taki, Moriyama Mayumi, and Akamatsu Ryōko;[3] anthropologist

---

1   *Yume wa toki o koete: Tsuda Umeko ga tsumuida kizuna* [A Dream across Time and Place: The Legacy of Tsuda Umeko], ed. Eiga Shinario Taiyaku Sakusei Projekuto [Translation Project for the Film Script] (Tsuda College, 2003), 143.

2   In the old system. In today's system, it would correspond to a high school.

3   Akamatsu was head of the Women's Bureau of the Ministry of Labor when the Equal Employment Opportunity Law was enacted.

Nakane Chie, the first woman to become a professor at the University of Tokyo; and Ikawa Fumiko, who became an associate vice-president of Canada's McGill University. Moriyama is, to date, the only woman to serve as Japan's chief cabinet secretary.

Thus, Tsuda Umeko's status as an important historical figure is due to more than just her pioneering work in higher education for women. The achievements of the alumnae of her school have served to enhance her standing. The impressive succession of high-achieving alumnae was made possible in part by the foresight and enterprise of the founder in preparing a solid foundation that ensured the continuation of her school for the next 120 years. To further elucidate this point, I will draw upon Chapter 8, which is titled "Connections."

Umeko was in her mid-twenties and a teacher at the Peeresses' School in Tokyo when she decided that she wanted to study abroad again in order to become a top-quality educator. She asked the advice of Mary Morris, whom she knew from her first stay in America. Morris spoke to the president of Bryn Mawr College, who made it possible for Umeko to be exempted from tuition and dormitory fees. She chose to study biology—a scientific field not recommended for women in those days in Japan—and she worked with T.H. Morgan, who later received the Nobel Prize in Physiology or Medicine.

After two years of intensive study at Bryn Mawr, Umeko requested a one-year extension. The main purpose of the extension was to establish a scholarship fund. She hoped to share her valuable experience in higher education by extending the same opportunity to other Japanese women, and if she could collect 8,000 dollars, the interest would permit one student to be dispatched every four years to study at Bryn Mawr College. Morris, who had helped Umeko to go abroad for a second time, and M. Carey Thomas, who was dean of Bryn Mawr and Umeko's mentor during her time there, assisted wholeheartedly in her fundraising. They succeeded in collecting the target sum in one year and the American Scholarship for Japanese Women came into existence.

The list of students who were awarded this scholarship includes many women who became outstanding leaders. The first recipient was Matsuda Michi, who graduated from Bryn Mawr in 1899 and became principal of Dōshisha Women's College in Kyoto. The second was Kawai Michi, who graduated in 1904 and established Keisen Jogakuen (Keisen Girls' School) in Tokyo. She was also the first general secretary of the Japanese YWCA. The fourth recipient was Hoshino Ai, who graduated from Bryn Mawr in 1912. Hoshino taught at Tsuda College after returning to Japan, became deputy head in 1925, and was instrumental in rebuilding the school after the devastation of the Great Kantō Earthquake. When Tsuda Umeko passed away in 1929, Hoshino became the second president of the school and took on the burden of being Tsuda's successor. As evidenced in her actions during the "Plaque Incident" mentioned in *Tsuda Umeko*, Hoshino capably steered the school through the difficult Pacific War years when English was regarded as an enemy language, all while navigating the dire financial situation caused by the decrease in students. After the war, she reorganized the infrastructure of the school when it was officially designated as Tsuda College and stayed on as president until 1952. These manifold achievements place Hoshino in the position of a "second founder." Fujita Taki, who headed the college from 1962 to 1973, was the seventh recipient of the scholarship. After graduating from Bryn Mawr in 1925, in addition to later becoming president of Tsuda College, she served as the second director of the Women's and Minors' Bureau of the Ministry of Labor and was a Japanese delegate to the United Nations.

Kawai Michi and Hoshino Ai were members of the Education Reform Committee, a GHQ-backed group established during the American Occupation of Japan. They were the only two women among thirty-eight members. Having lived through years of deteriorating relations between

Japan and the U.S., now at last, half a century after the founding of the American Scholarship for Japanese Women, they were in a position to negotiate on an equal basis with the Americans.

The American Scholarship for Japanese Women was sustained until 1976 and enabled twenty-five students to study in the U.S. The one-year fundraising campaign that Umeko initiated in 1891 resulted in numerous women being given valuable educational opportunities. Some of them subsequently dealt with unprecedented crises like the Great Kantō Earthquake and the Pacific War as they carried on and expanded the small private school that Umeko had founded. Her success in establishing the scholarship was one of the factors that enabled her to take the bold action of resigning from the Peeresses' School in 1900 in order to found Tsuda College. This is because some of the contributors to the scholarship fund also supported her plan to establish a private school. In retrospect, Umeko was building a network of connections a decade before she actually founded the school.

In an era when Japanese colleges closed their doors to women students, Umeko looked to American women for help and received it. She created a global network that enabled Japanese women to obtain an advanced college education in the U.S. She herself had a rare educational opportunity, but she did not let the opportunity end as a "dot in time." She ensured that the "dot" would become a "line" that went on and on. Another result of her efforts is that ten of the eleven presidents of the Tsuda school have been women, including myself. This high percentage is very rare in Japan. At Tsuda University, we refer to the idea of passing on one's experiences and opportunities to the next generation as the "Tsuda Spirit."

Even today, in 2020, Japan lags far behind other nations in the participation of women in society. The Global Gender Gap Report of 2020 ranks Japan in 121st place among 153 nations. To compete equally with the rest of the world, we must find a way to nurture innovative women leaders. We of the twenty-first century have much to learn from the resolve shown by Tsuda Umeko, a woman born at the end of the Edo period. And we can learn from the "life behind the words" how she "poured her soul" into teaching.

At this point, I would like to refer to a talk given by Ōba (which we have a recording of in our audiovisual center) and consider her motivation in writing this book. Ōba was a graduate of Tsuda College and one of its highest achievers. On October 10, 1987, she spoke at the college's Homecoming Day, when alumnae of the school come together to renew old friendships. The title of her talk was "What I Remember." Around this time, Ōba had begun to read Umeko's letters that form the basis of the book, and she was mulling over in her mind whether to accept the invitation to write it.

Ōba wove memories of her own college years into Umeko's story, and in her talk, she mentioned two major reasons for choosing Tsuda College. The foremost reason was the dormitory, where students from all prefectures were accepted. Regarding the second, Ōba said: "I think a major reason I chose this school was that it had a policy of education, based on the ideas of founder Tsuda Umeko, that focused on English—which was back then, and still is today, I believe, the representative language of the Western world—and it conducted this education in very small classes, similar to "juku" as the school name suggests." (In Japanese, Tsuda College was known as "Tsuda Juku." A "juku" is a small, private tutoring school.)

The lecture continued with "language" as a key word, beginning with Umeko's difficulty with the Japanese language when she returned to Japan, and going on to describe Ōba's difficulty with English at the beginning of her eleven-year sojourn in Alaska, in the United States. She compared the two experiences and declared that she knew exactly how Umeko must have felt. Umeko's experience of a strange culture coincided with her own, and Ōba suggested that going to a foreign country and learning a foreign language was a way of "discovering one's own self." She further remarked that "Learning English is, of course, a way to understand Western culture, but at the same time, learning a language that is completely different from your own is also a way to discover Japanese culture, to encounter it in a different way..."

Ōba probed Tsuda Umeko's intentions to gain an understanding of what she hoped for in founding a school. She believed Umeko felt that "learning a language is the quickest way to understand the thinking behind that language," and thus, that her ultimate goal was to teach those ways of thinking. After college, Ōba experienced eleven years of foreign culture living in Alaska, and I believe this to be an important element underlying her characterization of Tsuda Umeko. Ōba described her four years of dormitory life at Tsuda College as a "lifelong treasure." She noted that "I sometimes think I have been nibbling away at the legacy of those four years ever since—that this treasure has made it possible for me to survive."

In an essay titled "Tsuda Juku e no omoi" (Remembering Tsuda College),[4] Ōba referred to an episode that occurred when she received the Akutagawa Prize, a prestigious literary award for new writers. An excerpt from that essay is below:

> Seven years ago, when I received the Akutagawa Prize, Fujita-sensei, then president of Tsuda, sent me a congratulatory postcard that I was thrilled to receive. She wrote something like, "Although I won't say that it was Tsuda that made you, I am exultant." I wrote back right away: "No, I believe that it *was* Tsuda that made me. But one of these days, I may do something to make everyone connected to Tsuda very, very angry."
>
> Tsuda nurtured me in my youth. I was a rebel and a very poor student, but all the same, my time at Tsuda comprises a brilliant part of my life. What I am most grateful to Tsuda College for is that I

---

4   Included in Ōba Minako, *Onna no dansei ron* [Women Talking about Men] (Tokyo: Chūō Kōronsha, 1979), 136.

learned the "spirit of expressing individuality" on its campus. That is, I learned that we are free to express ourselves, but that we also have the responsibility to recognize the freedom of others. I was taught a good kind of individualism.

It must have been such positive memories of her student days that motivated Ōba's decision to take on this book. She mentioned the project in the following manner:

Recently I have been asked to write about Umeko, and I don't know how it will turn out, but I am a graduate of the school, and I am thinking that it will be nicer to read up on things that relate to me, rather than something that has nothing to do with me at all. I might find something new and make fresh connections. I haven't made up my mind. I've been reading various biographies, and reading her letters, but I never met Tsuda Umeko in person. I only know what she left us, and although there are a few people living who actually knew her and whom I can talk to, the rest will be a work of the imagination—of thinking "it must have been like that" or "it must have been like this." Writing a biography will be like writing a mystery novel. Yes, I think that is how it will be.

Ōba Minako brought Umeko to life on the basis of her letters. At the same time, Ōba was rediscovering her own college years and reliving the vibrancy of her youth. It was four years after the end of the Pacific War when she began her studies at Tsuda College. In the final chapter of *Tsuda Umeko*, she describes how Hoshino Ai, Umeko's successor, dealt with the "Plaque Incident" during the war and then shielded the school and its students during the postwar occupation.

Ōba was a student at Kamo Girl's Secondary School in Saijō (today part of Higashi Hiroshima city), Hiroshima prefecture, when the war ended.

An atomic bomb had been dropped on the city of Hiroshima on August 6, 1945, and Ōba and her classmates were sent into the city to help care for victims. They stayed for two weeks, from the end of August to the beginning of September and were witness to the horrible suffering of the injured. Ōba ends *Tsuda Umeko* with a description of the school in the mid-1940s, a time when the students and teachers were living through the war and the postwar occupation. I would like to make special mention of the fact that Ōba's personal experience of the devastation of war flows like an undercurrent through all that she writes.[5] This reminds me once again of how much the history of Tsuda College is entwined with the history of the relationship between Japan and the United States of America.[6]

Takahashi Yūko
September 2020

---

5   Egusa Mitsuko, *Ōba Minako no sekai: Arasuka, Hiroshima, Niigata* [The World of Ōba Minako: Alaska, Hiroshima, Niigata] (Tokyo: Shinyōsha, 2001), 225–26.

6   My comments on the education of women leaders and the American Scholarship for Japanese Women are reprinted here, with a number of additions and changes, from Takahashi Yūko, "Josei rīdā no ikusei to Tsuda Umeko" [The Education of Women Leaders and Tsuda Umeko], which was my preface to *IDE Gendai no kōtō kyōiku* [IDE-Higher Education Today], vol. 604 (Oct. 2018) published by the Institute for Development of Higher Education.

About the Author

Ōba Minako was born in Tokyo on November 11, 1930. She graduated from Tsuda College in 1953 with a degree in English literature, then married and moved to the United States in 1959 when her husband took a position as a chemical engineer in Sitka, Alaska. She and her family lived there until 1970.

In 1968, her debut novel, *Sanbiki no kani* (Three Crabs) won the Akutagawa Prize, a prestigious literary prize awarded to new authors, thus opening her way to a writing career. Apart from several dozen novels, she wrote essays, literary criticism, poetry, and a play, and co-edited a number of literary anthologies. She also translated children's books from English into Japanese and Japanese classics into modern Japanese.

Ōba was awarded numerous prizes, including the Women Writers' Prize for *Garakuta hakubutsukan* (The Museum of Odds and Ends) in 1975, the Tanizaki Prize for *Katachi mo naku* (Without Form) in 1982, the Noma Prize for *Naku tori no* (Of Birds Crying) in 1986, the Yomiuri Prize for Literature for *Tsuda Umeko* in 1990, and the Murasaki Shikibu Literary Prize for *Urayasu uta nikki* (Urayasu Poem Diary) in 2003. She played an active role in the Japanese literary world and served as the first female member of the Akutagawa Prize selection committee, vice president of the Japan P.E.N. Club, and head of the Women Writers' Association. She was elected to the Japan Art Academy in 1991.

A number of her novels and short stories have been translated into Western languages, including the novels *Three Crabs*, *Of Birds Crying*, and *Urashimaso* in English; *Träume fischen* and *Tanze, Schneck, Tanz* in German; and *L'île sans enfants* and *Larmes de princesse* in French.

Ōba Minako died on May 24, 2007. She was seventy-six years old.

About the Translator

Tani Yū has been a translator of fiction and nonfiction for many years. Books translated into English from Japanese include the novel *Urashimaso* by Ōba Minako. Books co-translated into Japanese from English include *Marxism and Totality* and *Refractions of Violence* by Martin Jay, and *The New Constellation* by Richard J. Bernstein. Tani is the daughter of Ōba Minako.

（英文版）津田梅子
Reflections on Tsuda Umeko: Pioneer of Women's Education in Japan

2021年3月27日　第1刷発行

著　者　　大庭みな子
訳　者　　谷 優
発行所　　一般財団法人出版文化産業振興財団
　　　　　〒101-0051 東京都千代田区神田神保町2-2-30
　　　　　電話　03-5211-7283
　　　　　ホームページ　https://www.jpic.or.jp/

印刷・製本所　　大日本印刷株式会社